Survival Kit for an Equity Analyst

Survival Kit for an Equity Analyst

The Essentials You Must Know

Shin Horie

WILEY

Library of Congress Cataloging-in-Publication Data

Names: Horie, Shin, author.
Title: Survival kit for an equity analyst : the essentials you must know / Shin Horie.
Description: Chichester, West Sussex, United Kingdom : John Wiley & Sons, 2022.
Identifiers: LCCN 2021031903 (print) | LCCN 2021031904 (ebook) | ISBN 9781119822448 (cloth) | ISBN 9781119822455 (adobe pdf) | ISBN 9781119822462 (epub)
Subjects: LCSH: Corporations—Valuation. | Business enterprises—Valuation. | Corporations—Finance. | Business enterprises—Finance. | Investment analysis.
Classification: LCC HG4028.V3 H67 2022 (print) | LCC HG4028.V3 (ebook) | DDC 658.15—dc23
LC record available at https://lccn.loc.gov/2021031903
LC ebook record available at https://lccn.loc.gov/2021031904

Cover Design: Wiley
Cover Image: © Tarchyshnik/Getty

Set in 11.5/14.5pt STIX Two Text by Straive, Chennai
SKY02BA45CC-597A-4B09-A1DB-3B1490BEEC90_101221

To Makiko, Waka and Hana

Contents

Preface: Why I Wanted to Write This Book

What do equity analysts do? When I was asked to explain what I do by my parents, who are not familiar with the financial industry, I told them: 'We try to predict the future of a company.' Simply put, that's what equity analysts do and, in my view, should be doing.

Talking about the past and the present is relatively straightforward. Talking about the future is more uncomfortable as no one likes uncertainty or being seen to be wrong in front of other people, which is why there is significant value in a quality attempt at predicting the future of a company. To do this, analysts need to understand many things that require a lot of research and investigation. This book provides equity analysts with a number of helpful hints and tools to help them navigate the complex research process, particularly when they are early in their careers.

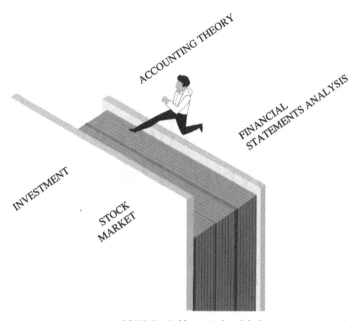

SOURCE: Goldman Sachs Global Investment Research

This is a book for company analysis, not a financial theory book, nor a business school textbook. It aims to be a practical guide on how to survive and thrive during the first few years as an equity research analyst. So, when I refer to 'we' or 'you' I am referring to new equity analysts. The book contains details of how to discover, analyse, forecast, and evaluate public companies. It has four unique features:

- First, it specifically focuses on company analysis and valuation and does not directly talk about stock investment, although the ultimate aim of our analysis is that the analysis is used for investment decisions. This focus is because we often make the mistake of talking about stock price movement before we fully understand the underlying company value and thus get confused between the two.

- Second, this book does not go into the theoretical definitions of accounting and financial analysis. This is because there are many textbooks available on this subject and most readers have already studied them extensively. Instead, I offer some suggestions and advice on how to implement such metrics in the real world of company analysis.

- Third, a number of specific industries are discussed because characteristics, growth prospects, and valuation methodologies vary substantially by industry. Readers can then apply the content directly to the industries they need to analyse.

- Fourth, by leveraging my background and experience, I tried to make the content as globally applicable as possible. As such, many parts of this book would also be relevant for emerging market analysts.

Introduction: How to Approach Company Analysis

When asked to analyse and value a company, the best starting point is not to start by punching its financial statements into a spreadsheet. In order to understand a company in a deeper manner, we need to: start with an in-depth analysis of the industry it belongs to; look at it in a global context; and learn about its competitors. We need to come up with our own 5–10-year outlook for the industry. During this process, in addition to investigating various data, we also need to speak with a number of industry experts, including the company's suppliers and customers, or even regulators or scientists in some cases. Then we take a detailed look into the company itself, more specifically regarding its history, management, shareholders, culture, and competitive moat – i.e. the 'personality' of a company.

When learning about the company, we need to undertake extensive interviews with senior management and the heads of its major businesses. Factory and store visits, or evaluating mines and project sites first hand, are also critical parts in the overall process. Once all the ingredients are ready, we can combine our insights with the earnings forecasts. These forecasts are not just a linear extension of past growth rates and margins. Having foresight of non-linear structural change is the real value addition of company analysis. Only then do we put a value on the company. At this stage, we need to leverage the market price on top of fundamental financial data. There are many different types of valuation methodologies depending on the nature of the business. The process is more of an art than a science and we need to be flexible and creative to aim at being roughly right rather than precisely wrong. At the end of this process we gauge if our view is different to the market consensus or not. If we have a differentiated view, we need to identify and articulate where and why we are different.

Structure of this Book

- **PART I: My Story**
- **PART II: Laying the Groundwork**
  - Chapter 1 introduces six basic steps to forecast industry TAM growth and then 10 additional considerations to help identify the 'character' of an industry.
  - Chapter 2 provides useful guidelines on the 'earnings drivers' in different industries.
  - Chapter 3 assists in identifying the 'personality' of a company.

- **PART III: Analyse and Apply the Findings**
  - Chapter 4 discusses how to combine all the accumulated knowledge and insights to produce financial forecasts.
  - Chapter 5 explains how a scorecard can be used to summarize and digest what has been learnt and forecast.
  - Chapter 6 aims to provide a framework for analysts to value companies in different sectors based on the fundamentals.
  - Chapter 7 provides structure on how to think about differentiated views versus the street.
- **PART IV: What to Research and How to Power the Analysis**
  - Chapter 8 provides suggestions on how to generate exciting new research ideas.
  - Chapter 9 addresses some specific issues such as Disruptors, Emerging Markets, Environmental, Social, and Governance, and Downturns.
  - Chapter 10 suggests a number of soft skills that can be used to power the analysis.
- **PART V: Recap and Closing Thoughts**

If the whole book has been read, a new analyst will have a detailed overview of the company research process. But what I am really hoping, as an author, is that analysts keep this book on their desks and refer to specific sections when they run into issues during their own researching process, and that they find something useful within the book to help navigate these issues.

I purposely avoided the use of specific company names and industry data throughout the book because what I want to discuss is the process of doing research as opposed to my directional view on specific industries or companies. However, all the examples used in the book are actual cases I have encountered.

Although this book is written mainly for equity analysts researching public companies, I would be delighted if private equity investors and managers in corporate strategy also find some parts of the book useful.

Before we get into the methodologies of company analysis, I would like to start with my own experience as an equity research analyst, which contains a number of real-life examples of the issues that are discussed in later chapters. However, if you need practical advice immediately, you can go straight to Chapter 1 and visit my story later.

List of Acronyms

1P	First-party relationship
3P	Third-party relationship
ABS	Acrylonitrile Butadiene Styrene
ADR	American Depository Receipt
AI	Artificial Intelligence
AP	Accounts Payable
AR	Accounts Receivable
ARPU	Average Revenue per User
B2B	Business-to-Business
CAC	Customer Acquisition Cost
CAGR	Compound Annual Growth Rate
CAMEL	Capital, Asset Quality, Management, Earnings, and Liquidity
CEO	Chief Executive Officer
CFO	Chief Financial Officer

CMO	Contract Manufacturing Organization
CMOS	Complementary Metal-Oxide Semiconductor
CNC	Computer Numerical Control
COGS	Cost of Goods Sold
CPU	Central Processing Unit
CROCI	Cash Return on Capital Invested
DACF	Debt Adjusted Cash Flow
DCF	Discounted Cash Flow
DDM	Dividend Discount Model
DeFi	De-Centralized Finance
DM	Developed Markets
DRAM	Dynamic Random Access Memory
EBIT	Earnings Before Interest and Taxes
EBITDA	Earnings Before Interest, Taxes, Depreciation, and Amortization
EM	Emerging Markets
EPS	Earnings per Share
ESG	Environmental, Social, and Governance
ESOP	Employee Share Ownership Plan
EU	European Union
EV	Enterprise Value
EV/EBITDA	Enterprise Value/EBITDA
FCF	Free Cash Flow
Fintech	Financial Technology
GAAP	Generally Accepted Accounting Principles
GCI	Gross Cash Invested
GDP	Gross Domestic Product
GMV	Gross Merchandise Value
GPU	Graphics Processing Unit
GTV	Gross Transaction Value
IaaS	Infrastructure as a Service
IAS	International Accounting Standards

IPO	Initial Public Offering
ITPC	International Trade Partners Conference
KOLs	Key Opinion Leaders
LCD	Liquid Crystal Display
LiDAR	Light Detection and Ranging
LNG	Liquefied Natural Gas
LTV	Life Time Value
M&A	Mergers and Acquisitions
MAU	Monthly Active Users
MLCC	Multilayer Ceramic Capacitors
NAV	Net Asset Value
NFT	Non-Fungible Token
OLED	Organic Light-Emitting Diode
P&C	Property and Casualty
P/B	Price to Book
P/E	Price to Earnings
P/PPOP	Price to Pre-Provision Operating Profit
PaaS	Platform as a Service
PEG	Price Earnings to Growth
PET	Polyethylene Terephthalate
PVC	Polyvinyl Chloride
R&D	Research and Development
REIT	Real Estate Investment Trust
REITs	Real Estate Investment Trusts
ROE	Return on Equity
ROIC	Return on Invested Capital
SaaS	Software as a Service
SEMI	Semiconductor Equipment and Materials International
SiC	Silicon Carbide
SKU	Stock Keeping Unit
SNS	Social Network Service

SOTP	Sum of the Parts
SPE	Semiconductor Production Equipment
SVOD	Subscription Video on Demand
TAM	Total Addressable Market
VR	Virtual Reality
WACC	Weighted Average Cost of Capital

Part I

Lessons from the Past: My Story as an Analyst

I plan to draw on my 33-year career as an equity analyst to offer anecdotes that illustrate why the intellectual challenge of equity analysis never gets stale, and why starting with some basic tools is so valuable. Repeatedly throughout my career I have moved into a different research environment that required me to look at a new landscape; whether this was being assigned to cover the capital goods industry in Japan in the 1980s or serving as the first Japanese analyst covering China H-share companies in the 1990s, the essentials were the same. What were the core characteristics of the industries and the sources of structural change? Who were the players and what was the distinguishing 'personality' of each? What were its earnings drivers and how were those changing against the industry backdrop? Finally, where did that mean the numbers were going and what were investors missing?

From Fish Cakes to Computer Numerical Control (1988–1995)

Anyone who has ever eaten a California roll at their local sushi place is familiar with surimi. But you have probably never given a thought to where the white, flaky 'imitation crab' meat comes from. I hadn't either until one day in 1988 when I was given my first assignment as a new equity analyst at Nomura Research Institute to analyse one of the top Japanese fishery companies. The pelagic fishery industry had been one of the major industries in Japan in the early twentieth century, and most companies made significant profits from it. After the 1960s, given the international pressure to ban whale fishing, fishery companies had to seek other sources of profit. Surimi, the fish cake, was a promising next pillar of profit growth.

When I was assigned to research the company, my supervisor told me to collect 50 name cards from the company before I started to write the report. It was not easy to come up with reasons to meet that many people in one company, hence I had to study thoroughly the company's products, its organizational structure, production, marketing, research and development (R&D), and financials. I read many books regarding corporate management and studied its competitors. By the time I had collected 30 name cards, I found that the relatively new innovation of the 'Surimi Ship' was the source of its future growth, and I was fascinated by the concept. Surimi is made out of cod fish, but the fish does not keep its freshness for long so the company decided to set up a surimi production factory on board, processing the cod fish while the ship was returning from the trip. Although it was a significant capital expenditure burden for the company, the differentiated technology gave it a sustainable, profitable business. To study the technology and its patents, I needed to visit the National Diet Library and the Ministry of Agriculture, Forestry and Fisheries several times in addition to company interviews (the internet did not exist then!). I felt I did almost everything an outsider could do to study the company. The only thing I thought I missed was to actually board the surimi ship, which the company politely declined when I asked.

Although profitability of the surimi business could be influenced by fluctuations in price, I had a strong conviction that the company had a structural competitive moat in its profitable surimi business. Hence, my confidence level in my earnings growth forecasts for the company was very high. I am still thankful to my supervisor who pushed me and allowed me to go as deep as possible to learn about one company for my first assignment as an equity analyst. As I was so junior at that time, I had less expertise in translating this extensive knowledge of the fishery company into a smart investment idea. As my first encounter with a company as an equity analyst, I learnt many invaluable lessons. Spending so much time researching one company gave me a real sense of how a large corporation operates in the real world, such as how various organisational functions work, how the chief executive officer's (CEO) strategy is cascaded down, how financial budgets are determined, the motivations of employees, and whether conflicts of interest exist between divisions, and different layers of leadership. As analysts become more senior and become busier, they tend to see a company as a stock or a financial instrument (an important perspective for investors), but it is helpful for analysts to remind themselves of the human elements behind the financial figures. Even now, more than 30 years later, when I think about the potential behaviour or decision-making process of a large company, what I learnt from this initial company analysis provides me with a benchmark of my thoughts.

After the fishery industry, I was assigned to cover the capital goods industry. I absolutely loved the sector and visited companies that manufacture products such as bearings, fire engines, tractors, industrial pumps, heat exchangers, knitting machines, and automated diaper assembling equipment. Every company had its own history and a strong sense of pride in its product. As such, when I showed my sincerity and eagerness to learn about their business, they were very generous with their time. I learned new things every day and even started to like the smell of machine oil. I still remember the factory head of a major bicycle parts company commenting that they supplied some critical car parts to a top automotive company with only minimum profit. Although the company was the dominant player in the bicycle parts industry globally and very profitable, they kept the less profitable car parts business to keep up with 'major league' manufacturing technologies. The company is still the dominant player in their field today.

I sometimes made a terrible stock call. One day I found an interesting short article about 'low-cost CNC' in a machine tool industry magazine. Machine tools are used to curve metals into various shapes and are often called 'mother machines' because they produce core parts of other machines. There were many machine tool companies globally at that time, but the key component, CNC (computer numerical control: a dedicated computing unit and servo motors to control positioning of metal cutting tools), was largely supplied by one Japanese company. This CNC maker was highly profitable and had a disproportionate share of the industry profit pool while its customers, the machine tool makers, were suffering from low margins and significant earnings volatility. The magazine article talked about two start-up companies in California that had launched a substantially lower-priced CNC system operated by personal computers. I was very excited to read the article because those companies could totally reshape the machine tool industry structure through technology innovation.

My boss was generous enough to send me to the US West Coast to meet the founders of those private companies. Although I did not have an engineering background, I had studied CNC enough to hold a sensible conversation with them, and they took me seriously. The technology seemed to be legitimate and had a good track record of initial customer wins. The manufacturing facilities were modern and organized. I went back to Japan and cross checked what I had learnt with several industry engineers. Their feedback was generally favourable. So, with due diligence, I wrote a fairly pessimistic report regarding the future profitability of the dominant CNC company. I was completely wrong. The low-cost CNC stayed as a niche product and the dominant CNC company continued to grow their business very successfully and profitably. I learned a painful lesson. I was too excited about the initial idea of a dramatic shift in industry dynamics and did not pay enough attention to the multiple reasons why the incumbent had been so strong.

This was probably a typical case of 'confirmation bias'. I loved the story of small start-up companies potentially winning against a dominant large company and was almost unconsciously wishing such a market share shift to happen. So, I probably unconsciously selected to meet engineers who also wished the same result. Given the importance of the topic, I really should have solicited views from a more diverse group of experts.

Not Just a Japanese Tourist – Becoming a China H-share Analyst (1996–1998)

During my days as a backpacker in the mid-1980s, I spent about two months travelling around China when there were hardly any cars and thousands of bicycles on the street even in large cities. I was fascinated by the culture and people in this enormous country and felt the strong potential of the economy. Needless to say, I would never have predicted the country would come so far in terms of economic development. While I really enjoyed covering the capital goods industry where Japan had a very strong presence globally, I was looking for an opportunity to go to Hong Kong to get closer to Mainland China. At that time, most equity research activities related to Mainland China were done in Hong Kong. I went through extensive Mandarin language training for several months to prepare for the move. In 1996, the firm moved me to Hong Kong and I became the first equity analyst covering China H-shares with a Japanese passport. Back then, the concepts of an equity market and equity research were still in their early stages in Mainland China. Most listed companies at that time were state-owned enterprises and when I visited a power equipment company, my first interview as a China H-share analyst, the CEO gave me a 45-minute uninterrupted speech in response to my first simple question. By the end of it he hadn't answered my question either!

Despite some challenges, visiting countless number of companies and talking to management was an extremely rewarding experience. Many were at the very early stage of becoming commercial entities and were keen to learn from overseas companies regarding their internal organization, production, marketing, etc. As a non-local analyst with only a little local knowledge and connectivity, I tried to apply the basic global industry framework when analysing H-share companies. My assessment of the positioning of each company within the global competitive landscape was well received by investors not just regionally but globally too. Since I had spent a lot of time walking around factory floors of Japanese industrial companies, I was able to gauge the level of manufacturing proficiency of their Chinese counterparts by visiting the factories and asking a number of questions. At that time, many industries in China were extremely fragmented and I was able to provide insight into their potential consolidation process by leveraging the experience of developed markets. I was extremely happy to find that such skillsets gained through analysing Japanese and global capital goods companies was, and still remains, helpful to those investing in the China market. Although I was not aware of the concepts then, this was probably my first real attempt to use 'time machine' and 'pattern recognition' analysis that is discussed in Chapter 1. The fact that such tools were so powerful that even an analyst who was very new to China coverage was able to differentiate and add value almost immediately was a valuable lesson. Although I felt an extreme bull on Chinese industrial development at the time, in hindsight I was actually very conservative in my projections.

A Truly Global Research Experience – Semiconductor Analyst (1998–2007)

Having covered China H-share companies for three years I felt like testing my skills as an analyst on a truly global platform. In 1998, I was fortunate enough to join the Goldman Sachs technology research team covering the Japanese semiconductor industry. Since I knew nothing about semiconductors, I spent the first several months in the New York office learning the basics of the industry and getting connected with the US team. It was an incredible environment for me to learn from the 'all-stars' of technology research. One thing that really surprised me was the level of respect and attention research analysts and major investors received from corporate top management. Back then in Asia, investor relations was something corporates broadly treated as a low priority job, certainly not a necessity. Hence, analysts in Asia needed to make substantial efforts to establish 'give-and-take' relationships with corporate management before they were fully open to you.

After spending a super-exciting several months in New York, I went back to Tokyo and initiated coverage on the Japanese semiconductor equipment companies and also some technology hardware companies. The Japan sell-side community then was well established and produced high-quality research products, but it was also pretty domestic and a closed world. As a newcomer with only limited knowledge of the technology industry, I introduced two simple practices that immediately captured the attention of investors. One was the focus on quarterly earnings and the other was the timely read-across notes from the earnings calls of overseas companies. Those are pretty standard practice now but back then very few Japanese analysts were able to understand the nuance of earnings calls of US companies. Most sell-side analysts at that time were mainly focused on the annual earnings forecasts and did not adjust earnings forecasts frequently. In addition, the concept of street consensus earnings did not yet clearly exist. Such focus on very short-term earnings trends was adopted quickly in the Japanese market. Ironically, Japan probably had a high proportion of quality sell-side analyst reports, with in-depth discussions on corporate strategies and long-term structural industry perspectives, before the focus on short-term earnings kicked in.

After initiating on the Japanese technology companies, I spent the majority of my time on field trips. The technology hardware industry is global, interconnected, and fast moving, so travelling around the world and meeting various companies in the supply chain gave me a substantial information edge. To understand the semiconductor industry better, you need to understand all parts of the chain, including materials, equipment, components, devices, and the various final products such as personal computers (PCs), mobile phones, communication equipment, consumer electronics products, and autos. In addition, inventory levels of components and final products can fluctuate a lot. Pricing of memory chips such as dynamic random access memory (DRAM) and NAND flash memory can be very volatile. Chip makers introduce new process technologies every year to improve chip density. At that time there were also numerous mergers between chip makers and equipment makers. On average I was on the road about one-third of the time travelling between Mainland China, Taiwan, Korea, Netherland, and Silicon Valley, etc.

It was my dream come true in terms of global research. I exchanged multiple emails and phone calls each day with my global analyst counterparts in the United States, Taiwan, Korea, Europe, and Japan, sharing details of new findings. It is blindingly obvious now to connect Asian countries together but back then research teams were structured on a by-country basis. We were probably one of the first to create a fully functional Pan-Asia technology research team among sell-side research houses. Many people from the strategy divisions of global technology companies would come regularly to see us to garner our thoughts on the broad industry because even large technology companies did not have such a comprehensive understanding of the whole technology hardware industry on such a real-time basis.

One of the most memorable experiences for me was the International Trade Partners Conference (ITPC), organized by industry association SEMI (formerly Semiconductor Equipment and Materials International) and held annually in Hawaii. ITPC was initiated by SEMI in the 1980s, after the semiconductor trade dispute between the United States and Japan, in order to create a venue where global semiconductor top executives could get together to discuss the future of the industry. I was invited to the conference several times as a speaker and the experience gave me an invaluable industry network. Many top executives from the semiconductor industry were open, frank, collaborative, and willing to take feedback. Learning about their ambitions, strategies, and concerns at a beachfront bar in Maui Island, while also receiving questions about my views on the future direction of the industry and specific companies from chairpersons and CEOs, was a truly amazing experience. Observing how corporate executives interact with each other was not something analysts got to see often at that time and it was very educational. It was also good to meet some of their family members. In order to maintain this industry network, I sent my published research work regularly to those top executives. My list of contacts, across the globe, became as large as 2,000 at its peak, quite some progress on the 50 name-card goal I was set when first starting out as an equity analyst.

Another memorable research project was about ink jet printer cartridges. When we buy a personal printer, we tend to spend more money on the cartridges as consumables than the hardware and hence for printer manufacturers the majority of their profit comes from selling cartridges. Given these cartridges were heavily protected by patents and a high level of manufacturing process technology, there was no low-cost competition from Taiwan, Korea, and Mainland China then, unlike that faced by other technology products. Sustainability of the competitive edge makes a significant difference to the future profitability for printer makers. Given the high profitability, there were a number of companies entering into the third-party cartridge and refill market to capture the lucrative profit pool. At the same time, the European Union (EU) was investigating the printer cartridge market based on anti-trust concerns. But companies were not particularly vocal about this issue. As such, I needed to do something beyond regular research. I called some of my contacts who supplied materials and parts to the cartridge industry. I then met second- and third-tier printer makers in Taiwan and Korea and the producers of third-party cartridges. I also read patent filings and sought advice from a patent lawyer to learn about cross-licensing agreements. By the end, although there were no clear-cut answers, I concluded that inkjet cartridge technology was resilient enough to stay profitable for the time being. I had learnt my lesson though from the CNC case and tried a more balanced and less rushed approach to the research. Printer makers at that time were saying the cartridge business was resilient because they had a technology advantage but they provided little detail beyond that. So, my extra-mile research effort was very well received, particularly by long-term investors who held large positions in printer companies. Even now ink jet cartridges continue to be profitable and a major source of earnings for printer manufacturers.

New Lexicon: Clinical Trial, Cap Rate, Embedded Value, Metal Spread (2008–2013)

In 2008, I passed on my coverage to a colleague and became the Director of Japan Equity Research. On top of all the personnel-related matters, one of the main responsibilities of the Director of Research is quality control of the research product. From day one, for all analysts in Japan, I was required to give advice and approval for rating changes, new thematic reports, and coverage initiations via the Investment Review Committee. I had spent the previous 10 years thinking in depth about semiconductors and hardware technology, and had only limited ideas about other industries. There were many unusual words, such as cap rate, embedded value, phase three clinical trial, and metal spread. I needed to digest and study. Sometimes I spent hours discussing the dynamics of certain industries with analyst teams until midnight. It was a fascinating experience and I felt like a whole new area of my brain not previously used had been turned on.

Having attended these Investment Review Committee meetings for a few months, I was getting used to giving advice to real industry experts on their investment views. I found it absolutely fascinating to see that even 10-year or 15-year industry veterans have blind spots. As they know the industries so well and are deeply wedded to the sectors, they could sometimes miss some of the more obvious future trends. For example, when I was an analyst, a mistake I made in hindsight was being too slow to acknowledge the disappearance of film cameras and then also the decline of dedicated digital cameras. Since I knew how quickly the specifications of CMOS (complementary metal-oxide semiconductor; essentially the eye of the digital camera) image sensors and lens technologies had been progressing as a semiconductor analyst, I should have predicted the major decline of digital cameras earlier.

In a similar vein, discussions with the auto sector analysts on electric vehicle transition were also interesting. Auto-sector analysts have often said in the past that the pure electric vehicle adoption would likely be slow because the batteries are too heavy and too expensive, and automakers did not want to focus on this business because it was loss making. But I argued that I had seen many technologies advance faster than expected when the whole industry focused their efforts on it, and also it is ultimately the consumer who decides what to buy, not the car makers. While I don't think I always get the advice right, listening to the analysts present their high-level views and quickly identifying the blind spots without knowing too much detail is an extremely valuable skill I learned through the experience. I really wished I had listened to presentations by other analysts more when I was a coverage analyst and figured this out earlier.

During my tenure as the Director of Japan Equity Research, Japanese equity was not popular with investors – low profitability, slow to implement changes, poor corporate governance, and fierce competition from the rest of Asia. One day in 2010, when I went to see a client in Edinburgh, Scotland that was known for long-term selective investing, the veteran portfolio manager told me that our research was useless because it did not address the core value of a company at all. Hence, he gave no business to us. He said he was only interested in Japanese companies that he could buy, forgot about for five years, and that would outperform the market. I went back to Japan, discussed with our analyst population and decided to launch a 'Japan 2020' series. This research series was basically to select several companies in Japan where the analysts felt strongly about sustainable growth potential in the next 10 years and then undertook a deep dive on the industry structure analysis and prepared 10-year financial projections. Some reports took almost six months to prepare and the research team successfully published a number of Japan 2020 reports in the following 12 months. Those reports were very well received, in particular by overseas investors who had historically disliked Japanese equities. The corporates also appreciated our efforts. It was a great learning tool for our analysts to go beyond the normal forecast time horizon. A year later, I went back to Edinburgh to see the same portfolio manager and I was very pleased to find he had read all of the Japan 2020 reports in detail.

Importing DM Experience to EM: From Japan to Asia-Pacific (2014–2017)

When my immediate boss in Hong Kong retired, I was asked to run the Asia-Pacific equity research department with a very talented British colleague. Even though I had experience in Korean, Taiwanese, and Mainland China markets through my technology research, I lacked confidence that I could lead the complex Asia-Pacific region with 11 offices and 13 different markets. Although I would not characterize the transition as easy, it was a lot smoother than I anticipated. Many of the skills and experience I had accumulated as an analyst in Japan readily transferred to other markets. With a little sensitivity towards cultural differences, the process of training junior analysts and motivating senior analysts was surprisingly similar in different countries, not easy but similar.

Even more pleasing, I found I was able to help analysts deepen and broaden their thoughts on a number of industries in emerging markets (EM) by providing my experience from developed markets (DM). When we wanted to analyse the future of the convenience store business in Thailand and Taiwan, we had to study the history of the industry in Japan and Korea in detail. If we need to have a 20-year vision of the supermarket business in India, we have to study US supermarkets in the 1970s. Japanese furniture chain stores could give us strong insights into the future of Chinese furniture makers. When we wanted to conduct long-term steel demand forecasts for India, it was very insightful to compare 'steel intensity' (consumption of steel versus GDP) across various different countries. It sounds a very basic thing to do but I was surprised to find not many analysts in these growth markets spent sufficient time learning from the histories of developed markets.

When I started to lead the Investment Review Committee in Japan and to deal with the industries I was unfamiliar with, I needed to develop the skills to pick up the salient points quickly without knowing all the detail. Having been involved in the Japanese equity market for almost 20 years by then, if I heard the name of the major listed companies, I at least had a rough idea of what they all did. But when my remit expanded to Asia-Pacific, I could not even pronounce the names of the majority of companies. It was not easy to provide sensible advice to improve the quality of analysis and to avoid pitfalls just listening to 20–30-minute presentations about companies I had never heard of.

The tools that helped me substantially during this learning period included 'time machine analysis' and 'pattern recognition analysis'. Time machine analysis simply compares development of the same industry across different countries. Pattern recognition compares different industries in different counties with similar industry dynamics. For example, an analyst wanted to argue that Chinese steel companies would go through a consolidation phase as a result of the regulations linked to severe emission requirements, and that this would result in less earnings volatility and higher stock valuations. However, while there were no obvious examples in the steel industry to illustrate the impact of these changes, the hard disk drive industry in the United States had been through similar changes in the past. So, the analyst was able to study the dynamics of the hard disk drive industry over several years and see whether there were any similarities with the Chinese steel industry. Although none of these analysis tools can make a perfect magic mirror, they can give provide a bit more conviction to our view.

The import substitution theme in the Chinese market was another really interesting example of leveraging DM knowledge to EM. When I was visiting China regularly as an analyst during the period 2000 to 2008, China was already widely known as 'the factory of the world' and was manufacturing a variety of products to export to global markets. But the factory managers I met often said that while they were able to source most of the basic parts from China, certain key components and materials had to be sourced from Japan or Europe, which prevented them from further cost reduction. Following that, I started to notice some Chinese companies gradually localizing the manufacturing of such key parts and materials, while at the same time the government was pushing the upgrading of manufacturing industries. I thought it would become a prevailing growth theme and looked for companies who would benefit from this shift. One good recent example as a continuation of this theme was a manufacturer of hydraulic components used for construction machinery. The Chinese company basically produced a similar quality of hydraulic components with a lower cost compared to Japanese companies and thus has steadily replaced the latter in the Chinese market over the past several years.

Unlike developed markets, small–mid cap coverage is generally very thin in growth markets, especially among global research houses. Hence, finding attractive growth companies was a very effective way to identify alpha generation opportunities. This approach is particularly effective with the China A-share market (Chinese companies listed onshore in Mainland China) where the more than 3,000 companies currently listed operate in a full range of industries from services to manufacturing. Usually, those interesting growth companies are first discovered by local investors but increasingly foreign investors have the chance to find hidden jewels in certain areas such as low-profile specialized industrial products that may not be as fully appreciated by the local investor base. Some foreign investors have seen the industry dynamics and growth of very similar companies in their home markets and hence immediately understand the opportunities.

Connecting the Dots: From Asia to Global (2018–now)

After leadership changes, I was given the opportunity to cohead the Global Equity Research department with a US-based colleague. My cohead used to be one of the legendary 'all-star' technology analysts in the US market and it was very natural for him to lead the global team from the headquarters in New York. So, I defined my role as 'connecting the dots', with the aim of substantially improving our global connectivity between analysts. Taking key advantage of my position in Asia, I put a strong emphasis on educating non-Chinese analysts about China and in turn educating Chinese analysts about the global situation and read-across for their companies.

Many industry teams already host regular global calls and frequently share information. But I did find that in many cases the analysts did not heavily debate and reconcile their disagreements because they did not want to step on the toes of other analysts. It is acceptable to not reach full agreement on everything, but there is a lot of value to everyone in having a quality debate. It was fascinating to see the business model differences of the food-delivery business by country, but the analyst teams never quite fully understood these until they held in-depth global discussions on it. Auto-industry analysts in each region have different nuanced views regarding the electric vehicle adoption curve. Having an open debate on why they have different views is likely to be extremely beneficial to everyone in the global team.

It is also fascinating to find a perception gap across different markets. Even though we believe there is almost no time lag in accessing most investment related information, I was quite surprised to see a large perception gap on climate-control-related matters across different continents. Market participants and corporates in Europe were extremely serious about decarbonization of the economy and were taking various actions by 2018 when I first started this global research role. The US market, at least in my view, was substantially less sympathetic about CO_2 emission issues at that time and Asia was somewhere in between the United States and Europe. As of 2021, there are almost no regions or countries that are not serious about 'net-zero' emission efforts. So, if we were to have a full understanding of corporate actions, technology development, regulatory changes, and investor behaviour in Europe in 2018, and then if we had anticipated such changes in other markets, it would have provided a very successful investment in the past few years.

One thing I really enjoy and feel proud being part of is quick idea generation calls. This is when an analyst has a fresh important theme and then arranges a call with various relevant analysts across the globe to hold instant sophisticated discussions. It could be hydrogen energy, battery supply chain, 5G technology, US-China trade friction, tourism consumption, sportswear market, plant-based food, fintech, emission regulation on tankers, component shortage, or horizontal manufacturing model of the auto industry. I normally just listen or lightly moderate the discussion and am always fascinated to watch the process of real industry experts in different areas all contribute to create something very insightful. I have seen many cases where the collective minds of a small number of analysts have created a much larger impact than working solo.

In terms of analyst characters, I was quite surprised again to find substantially more similarities than differences among global analysts, a very similar experience to the one I had when shifting from Japan to Asia-Pacific. When I started the global role, I interviewed several of the most successful analysts in Europe and the United States about their success factors, with the list of answers almost amusingly similar to the ones I received from the top Asia analysts. It was particularly encouraging for me to have found all the top analysts strongly emphasized how much they enjoy the intellectual part of their work.

Part II

Laying the Groundwork

Chapter 1

Understand the 'Character' of the Industry

To forecast the medium-term outlook of a specific industry, analysts first need to understand its 'character'. It is particularly helpful to identify potential structural changes and the pace of these. Analysts can easily fall into a trap of simply extending the current status quo and calling it a forecast. To avoid this it is necessary to add more 'non-linear thinking' into the forecasts. The six basic steps for forecasting industry total addressable market (TAM) growth are laid out in this chapter. To foster flexibility of thought and add structural changes into the forecast figures, ten additional considerations for use during discussions are also given as a means to test the forecast figures. Each section discussion includes some tips on how to gather such information. Although this part of the research process can be overwhelming given the information load, analysts should learn to go as broad and deep as possible to have maximum basic knowledge of the industry. However, it is equally important for analysts to consciously try to pick up two or three 'interesting', 'surprising', or 'counter-intuitive' findings from the research process.

Six Basic Steps for Forecasting Industry Growth

1: Product and Service Details

The first step when analysing industries is to fully understand the products and services that they provide. If it is a consumer-related product or service, every opportunity should be taken by the researcher to experience it first-hand. Understand clearly the details of the product such as usage pattern, unit price, production volume, pricing mechanism, manufacturing process, and supply chain. For highly technical areas, garner the help of industry experts, such as recently retired engineers from the relevant companies or university professors in the specific field, all of whom can be very helpful in gaining fundamental knowledge. Industry organizations or consulting firms focused on specific industries often provide crash courses on the industry basics for newcomers, which can be a very efficient way to learn about the industry in a short period of time. Factory and store visits are almost a 'must do' as they provide invaluable information analysts do not get from the data. Trade shows and industry conferences also offer a wealth of information, especially if dealing with some niche business-to-business type products that aren't normally encountered in everyday life. Industry trade shows in particular are ideal places to see products from all the major players and possibly attend some friendly tutorials given by marketing staff of the companies.

Extra caution should be taken when analysts work on new services or new businesses with popular concepts. When analysts use words such as artificial intelligence, internet of things, algorithm, value of customer data, and power of platform, they really need the ability to define exactly what those mean to the industry or the company being researched.

2: History of the Industry

Many industries are inter-related. It is often useful to investigate the history of the specific industry to understand its development through to its current structure. For example, it can be difficult to fully understand the software industry without studying the history of the computer industry. The long-term history of the auto industry, when hundreds of car manufacturers existed, can give us a good idea of how the electric vehicle industry could shape up over the next 10 years. Books and articles written by CEOs of relevant companies often contain a wealth of useful information. Experienced analysts have the advantage of knowing a lot of such history and context, but new analysts can leverage these books to compensate for any knowledge gaps. Some companies issue booklets on their corporate history that often contain useful nuggets of information. When visiting a company, especially manufacturing companies, the value of their showroom should not be underestimated as they often contain interesting hints to aid understanding of the nature of the industry. The showroom often demonstrates the evolution of key technologies with actual historical products and sometimes it even has conceptual prototypes of future products.

3: Definition of TAM and Segments

Before trying to forecast TAM growth, the product should be defined. If the categories being dealt with are large enough and well-defined, like autos and semiconductors, then those are straight-forward. But if the need arises to forecast special materials, machineries, or unique services, then those products or services need to be defined within the broader category, otherwise an analyst could miss structural changes occurring in the industry. Whether it is possible to analyse the video game console business in isolation or whether it needs to be discussed together with the mobile phone game market is a valid question. It is also important to think about both the merchant market and the internal market. For example, when thinking about the building maintenance business, the whole TAM size should include the services provided by third-parties and the services provided by building owners. If you are looking at the condiment market, then the business-to-business and business-to-consumer segments should be discussed separately. When analysing the titanium market, you need to take into account that pricing and demand for high-end aerospace grade titanium and other mid- to low-end grade titanium move very differently, and thus they should be treated separately. Many industries with significant import and export activities require a global view of TAM. As can be seen from these examples, the way TAM is defined will offer significant insight into the industry. Industry organizations normally provide detailed data as a starting point but sub-category industry data is not always readily available, especially for new industries. That said, the mosaic of third-party industry research data, statistics from industry organizations, and company disclosures, can all lead to a reasonable estimate.

4: Market Structure

Much of an industry's character is defined by the concentration of the market. Historical changes in market share and the nature of key players are also important considerations. Sometimes a competitor can also be a supplier, a customer, or a partner. Industries dominated by a regulated monopoly or state-owned enterprise have unique characteristics. Additionally, a fragmented market does not automatically lead to consolidation. Good graphical illustration of the industry structure and a supply chain map is very helpful for readers when explaining a complex industry. To understand the education business market, broad mapping needs to be done based on class size, average price, age group, online-offline mix, etc., because each player has different business domains and it is hard to compare them without knowing the big picture of the industry. The economic shock in 2020 caused by the Covid-19 pandemic provided an interesting lesson. Industries such as semiconductors have a narrow global supply chain that consists of highly specialized companies with high global market share that are scattered around the world. So, if something goes wrong with one company, the whole supply chain may have to stop operation. Such a supply chain is efficient and often profitable but also vulnerable. Alternatively, industries such as autos and consumer electronics, which source from multiple companies in their supply chain, can be less efficient but more resilient against any shocks.

5: Competitor Analysis

Understanding the character of key players in the market is critical. Suppose there are two identical industries, one with a very aggressive market consolidator and one without, the long-term industry profitability will be very different between the two. If the major competitor of a company is very focused on its profitability, an ugly price war is unlikely to happen in that industry. If a company is facing larger competitors, an analyst will need to study their potential weaknesses and gauge the possibility of market share gain. If the competitors are small, what needs to be monitored is whether the company has any disruptive new products or services. When looking at an industry where some major players are private companies, industry trade shows and conferences are good venues to meet such companies and actually experience the products. Funding conditions of those competitors can also significantly influence the industry's competitive dynamics as well, hence it is useful to look for their public filings on financial statements.

6: Global Comparison

This point cannot be emphasized enough. As a starting point of any industry analysis, if analysing an industry in a developed market, it is natural to compare it to similar ones in other developed markets. If looking at an industry in an emerging market, it should first be compared to similar ones in other emerging markets. While an analyst might think this part is unnecessary, especially if the subject industry is domestic in nature, it actually leads to a better understanding of that particular industry in Country A when a comparison is made with industries at a similar development stage in Countries B, C, and D. For example, unless comparing it with other countries of similar GDP per capita, you would not appreciate how far advanced Korea's online e-commerce market is. If there are any good examples, analysts can also look at developed markets to gauge the future development path. When analysing the convenience store business in Thailand, not only Taiwan and Korea but also Japan should offer good case studies for its future growth path. Analysts often just use the US market as a comparison because it has many listed companies and ample industry data, but it is better to use multiple countries for comparison purposes. To achieve this successfully, regular communication with peer analysts in other regions is critical. If such counterpart analysts are not available, alternative regular sources of information, such as specialized industry periodicals, can be used. You would not imagine that there is a monthly newsletter specializing in commercial fridges, but there is.

These steps are shown graphically for quick reference in Figure 1.1.

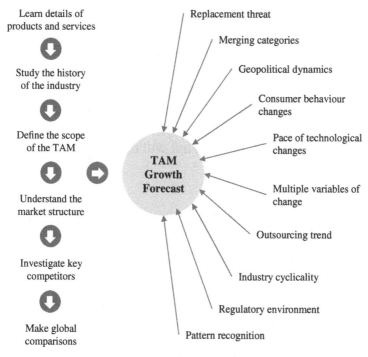

Figure 1.1   Steps to forecast industry growth
SOURCE: Goldman Sachs Global Investment Research

TAM Growth Rate

Once the six basic steps are completed, TAM growth can be forecast; this is the foundation of company analysis. Although ultimately the total TAM forecast figures consist of just 5 to 10 sets of dollar value numbers, assuming the forecast period is 5 to 10 years, these figures contain significant insights if completed properly. Some analysts just forecast TAM growth for two to three years, but in order to capture various structural changes of the industry a minimum of a five-year forecast horizon is necessary. A much deeper industry perspective is evident with five-year forecasts versus two-year

forecasts. Each industry has several growth drivers, such as penetration curve, affordability, pricing, innovation, demographics, consumer behaviour by cohort, industrial production growth, interest
rates, regulation, and environmental considerations. Collaboration
with other industry teams is critical as many forecast numbers are
dependent on one another. In situations where very limited public
industry data is available, an analyst may have to start with third-
party research industry forecasts but will need to do their own reality checks before using them.

Ten Additional Angles for Testing Forecasts

1: Replacement Threat from Other Businesses

Online retail is taking business away from traditional retail companies. Online payment is replacing cash. The smartphone is replacing
quartz watches. Even though movement is slow at the beginning,
once penetration reaches a certain level of traction, the market share
erosion can be very quick and non-linear. Ironically, quartz watches
replaced mechanical watches in somewhat the same way. Some
replacement threats are not as obvious as online retail but analysts
need to be alert to such possibilities. Unfortunately, management of
the companies who produce the products being replaced may often
recognize the seriousness of the threats too late, hence reliance on
conversations with the company could lead an analyst to draw the
wrong conclusions. Once it is identified that a certain business is
under serious threat, analysts should have the courage to reflect this
view into their long-term industry forecast figures.

2: Merging Categories

From time to time, really innovative companies can change the
landscape of the industry. Some smartphone makers are now generating more profit from their digital content distribution business

than from their handsets. Some capital goods companies are adding software solutions into their business model. Internet companies are moving into areas such as payment and lending, which have traditionally been under the umbrella of the financial services industry. The auto industry suddenly started to see new entrants in the market, which had not been seen for decades. E-commerce and advertising are crossing over. It certainly complicates the structure of the analysis but is a highly value-added part of the process if done well. Constant discussion with other sector teams and analysts, while also attending company presentations outside the assigned industry, could provide early signs of such a move. It is somewhat surprising to observe well-regarded and experienced senior analysts sometimes having fairly narrow viewpoints on their industry and missing the potentially bigger-picture structural changes.

3: Geopolitical Dynamics

Industry growth will be affected by various geopolitical issues. Trade disputes accelerate import substitution. Geopolitical economic sanctions and import tariffs can shift the sourcing of raw materials. Election results alter certain industrial policies substantially. Middle East tensions can have a significant impact on energy prices. As these issues are almost impossible to predict, framing the potential impact and running multiple scenarios based on different outcomes is a practical approach. Analysts should look at both the potential positive and negative impact from those incidents.

4: Consumer Behaviour Changes

Changes in consumer behaviour can materially impact industry dynamics. Consumption patterns of the Millennials and Generation Z cohorts have already impacted many industries. The ongoing emergence of Chinese, Indian, and African consumers is continuing to make a difference in the global consumer sector. Changes that could be seen in a post-Covid-19 world, such as broader digital technology adoption by the older population, location of offices, and health consciousness, are other obvious examples. Analysts often see things just from the viewpoint of the companies under coverage but it is also important to use a different lens – analysing things from the consumer's point of view.

5: Pace of Technology Changes

This is a difficult subject but highly value-added part of forecasting that an analyst cannot shy away from. Cost reduction of renewable energy has been changing the investment mix in the energy industry. Migration to a 5G mobile network can create a different competitive landscape for the whole supply chain. Improvement of LiDAR (light detection and ranging) technology could accelerate the adoption of autonomous driving. Analysts sometimes underestimate the magnitude of such changes, even though they are fully aware the changes are coming. In order to stay ahead of such early technology trends, analysts can check technical research papers, attend industry conferences, and speak with cutting-edge engineers. In particular, getting a sense of the technology progress and the time horizon as shared by leading scientists and engineers in these areas can be invaluable.

6: Multiple Variables

With a 5- or 10-year time horizon, a lot of things could change. When thinking about industry changes, analysts need to consider the improvement of multiple factors rather than just one. When visualizing the future of digital banking, we tend to think about the many new services that could be incorporated into the phone app but most of us assume we will be using the same smartphone hardware as we are today. But, in reality, there is a very good chance that the shape, form, and capability of the smartphone will be much more advanced. If so, the level of service a bank could offer may be considerably more sophisticated due to the changes in hardware. We do not know how smartphones will evolve or how digital banking services will progress over the next five years. It is not the job of the equity analyst to create a new business idea either. But the point here is to acknowledge that there is not just one single variable, instead multiple variables can affect each other, thus analysts should avoid linear thinking with a single variable.

AUTHOR ANECDOTE

In 1990, a technology analyst I greatly respected predicted that flat panel display (liquid crystal display, LCD) would become a US$10bn business and that NAND flash-based silicon audio would be a popular product in 10 years, even though neither was commercialized at that stage. He had carried out an incredible level of research on technology and demand forecasts. I was involved in the initial research discussion and frankly was a little sceptical about his super detailed bottom-up approach because this kind of approach often ended up being too detailed and losing sight of the big picture. However, the analyst continued to pursue the difficult path. He forecast the future demand of computers, TVs, and other displays where LCD would be used. He also forecast a detailed timeline on the production cost curve for each year. This was possible because he essentially knew all the major R&D engineers that were involved in the LCD business. Ten years later, he was spot on and I could not believe my eyes when I saw how accurate the original projection was. This is still one of the best examples I have seen of a well-researched bold estimate.

7: Outsourcing Trends

The outsourcing trends of corporates create new business segments – semiconductor foundry, software as a service, cloud services, India IT services, contract manufacturing organizations (CMO) in biotechnology, contract manufacturing of cosmetics products, private label foods, property management, distribution and logistics, staffing service, etc. A company that can create a de facto standard for certain processes can enjoy long-term sustainable growth but only a few players can be in that position. Outsourcing generally accelerates consolidation and improves industry efficiency. If you are a company providing such outsourcing services, you might be able to outgrow the TAM consistently. If you are the user of such outsourcing services, you might be able to narrow the technology or cost gap versus large companies who do not use the service. If you are one of the large incumbent players, you might lose part of the business. The semiconductor central processing unit (CPU) industry offers an interesting example of this. Significant changes in the auto supply chain would happen if electric vehicle makers started to adopt contract manufacturing models. It is useful to remind ourselves that even the computer industry, currently one of the best examples of an outsourcing industry model, started as a vertically integrated industry model with each maker having its own CPU, operating software, and hardware. The trend of using a shared central kitchen in the restaurant industry is another emerging example of outsourcing.

8: Industry Cyclicality

There are several cyclical industries and each has a unique characteristic. Capital goods exhibits a deeper but predictable economy-driven multi-year cycle. The cycle for commodities can be driven by more complex factors and the price moves can be more short term and volatile. Technology hardware is driven by the product cycle, technology cycle, and inventory cycle. The semiconductor industry cycle can be driven by supply and demand of memory devices and can be volatile. Analysts need to study the historical cycles of the industry. When forecasting for a cyclical industry, the option would be either explicitly add down years during the forecast period or discount the growth to avoid overestimation. This is discussed in more detail in Chapter 2 on earnings drivers.

9: Regulatory Environment

The level of regulation and changes in an industry can completely change the dynamics of that industry. The financial industry after the Global Financial Crisis in 2008 is one such example. Other examples include data privacy issues for internet companies, which changed the long-term trajectory of the industry, and changes in the tax policy on alcoholic beverages, which has had a significant impact on the industry. Constant checks on regulatory policy changes are important when looking at regulated industries. It is also important to bear in mind that these changes sometimes happen outside home countries.

10: Pattern Recognition

This is not an easy one for new analysts without long-term experience to master but it is a very useful tool. Pattern recognition here means when you need to predict the future outcome of Industry A in Country B, similar situations such as competitive dynamics, pricing environment, and regulatory changes for Industry C in Country D in the past can be used as a clue. For example, assume an analyst wants to research a restaurant chain in China that is successfully expanding its business by attracting young customers through a brand activism type of marketing method. To forecast the future outlook, the first step would be to find similar companies in the United States, Japan, or Europe for comparison purposes, but if this is not possible then examples in other industries, including sportswear, apparel, or even ice cream companies, could be studied to see how they develop their business through brand activism marketing. Such 'patterns' need to be picked carefully and be used with the knowledge that there are limitations on how far it can be extrapolated.

When making a comparison, the 'how to' on actually comparing two models is also important. If discussing whether the electric vehicle industry will shift to a horizontally integrated model in future, many analysts could easily come up with the idea of comparing it to the structure of the smartphone industry. But the real added value in this analysis is not just a simple comparison of production outsourcing percentage, but is instead a comparison of industry-wide profit pool shift and underlying incentives to pursue horizontal integration. When the mobile phone market shifted from feature phone to smartphone, the industry added significantly more utilities for users and hence created a new profit pool for phone makers. That partially drove the production outsourcing move seen in the smartphone industry. If similar dynamics were to happen in the electric vehicle industry, it might transition to a horizontal integration model.

Where to **start**   # What to **avoid**

Meet as many people as possible ✔	✘ Turning to the model too early – lay the groundwork first
Get on the road and visit ✔	✘ Linear thinking – analysts must understand change
Hit the history books ✔	✘ Narrow and local only viewpoint
Define TAM properly ✔	✘ Incumbent's cynicism
Use pattern recognition ✔	

SOURCE: Goldman Sachs Global Investment Research

Chapter 2

Assess the Earnings Drivers in Different Industries

Each industry generally has four or five key factors that drive the direction of revenue and earnings in both the short and long term. A good understanding of these earnings drivers makes the modelling process more efficient and improves an analyst's understanding of the company. Although the drivers are company specific and therefore not easy to generalize, this chapter provides useful sample guidelines on potential earnings drivers in major industries. Such drivers can change over time with industry environment changes and analysts should create their own version of the earnings drivers best suited for their coverage.

The industries in focus have been categorized by similar earnings patterns – hyper growth, secular growth, cyclical, cyclical growth, stable, interest rate sensitive, regulated, and conglomerates; Chapter 6 on valuation follows the same categorization. The name of each category is based on the view of developed markets in general. So, in a high-growth market, consumer staples companies could potentially have the earnings characteristics of the secular growth industry, for example, rather than the typical earnings characteristics as the 'stable' group where it is categorized in this chapter, given that that is how it is viewed in developed markets. The drivers are outlined briefly in Table 2.1 for quick reference.

Table 2.1 Earnings drivers in different industries

Industry and sub-segment	Drivers to watch
HYPER GROWTH	
Internet	• GMV growth • MAU growth • Time spent on the app • Monetization rate • Advertising spend • Customer acquisition cost • Regulatory changes
Fintech	• GTV growth • MAU growth • Financing cost • Credit provision • Average lending rate • Customer acquisition cost • Regulatory changes
Biotechnology	• Potential TAM of the drug • Approval process of the drug • Clinical data of the drug • News on competing drugs • M&A in the relevant area • Collaborations among key players

Industry and sub-segment	Drivers to watch
SECULAR GROWTH	
Software	• IT spending growth • Growth of the client's industry revenue pool • Client wins • Market share changes • Outsourcing trend of customers • Regulatory changes • New business models
Medical Technology	• Volume of patients • Volume of surgeries • Hospital capacity • Clinical data • Approval of new products • Regulatory changes • Hospital capex budget
CYCLICAL	
Capital Goods	• Demand in client's industries • Economic cycle, such as industrial production • Replacement cycle • Environmental regulation
Transport	• Passenger traffic • Fleet capacity • Fuel price • Cargo demand • Cost of financing

(Continued)

Table 2.1   *(Continued)*

Industry and sub-segment	Drivers to watch
Energy	• Crude oil price • Progress of exploration projects • Refiner demand and supply • Capex cycle
Commodities	• Underlying product demand and supply • Product inventories • Demand and supply of middle products and by-products • Disruption in mining operations
Chemicals	• End product demand • Price of feed stock • Product pricing • Production capacity expansion and utilization • Demand and supply of each manufacturing chain • Inventory level
Autos	• New model cycle • Gas prices • Consumer sentiment • Interest rates • Currency fluctuations • Emission regulation changes

Industry and sub-segment	Drivers to watch
CYCLICAL GROWTH Semiconductor	• Memory price cycle • Capex cycle • End product demand outlook • Product substitution • Process technology migration • Market share changes within category
Electronic Components	• End product demand outlook • Customer wins and losses • Inventory level • Product substitution
Technology Hardware (Enterprise)	• Customer spending • Technology migration • Product cycle • Customer wins and losses • Currency fluctuations
Technology Hardware (Consumer)	• New product cycle • Product pricing • Market share changes • Component costs • Currency fluctuations
Clean Energy	• Capex • Unit price reduction • Demand and supply • Energy price • Policy changes • Large new project launches

(Continued)

Table 2.1   *(Continued)*

Industry and sub-segment	Drivers to watch
STABLE	
Consumer Staples	• Consumption trend • Channel shift • Market share • Product pricing • Weather
Retail	• Store openings • Same store revenue growth • Increase in private label products • Competition from online • Development of new formats • Labour cost • Rental cost
Consumer Discretionary	• Product cycle • Demand cycle driven by the economy • Market share changes • Weather • Emerging market demand growth
Pharmaceutical	• Changes in TAM of major drugs • New drug approval process • M&A activities in the relevant areas • Healthcare policies
Media	• Consumer sentiment • Profitability of consumer companies • Content acquisition costs • Competition from online

Industry and sub-segment	Drivers to watch
Business Services	• Business trend of client's industry • Outsourcing trend • Competition • Cost inflation
INTEREST RATE SENSITIVE	
REITs	• Occupancy rate of underlying assets • Change in rental charges • Asset acquisitions • Change in financing cost • Government policy
Property Developers	• Unit sales • Unit pricing • Changes in cap rate • Landbank acquisition • Occupancy rate • Dividend pay-out • Financing cost • Government policy
Banks	• Industry data on loans and deposits • Interest rates • Capital levels • Liquidity management (loan and deposit ratios) • Interest rate risk management, duration, and rate sensitivity • Asset quality indicators and credit risk management • Regulatory changes

(Continued)

Table 2.1   *(Continued)*

Industry and sub-segment	Drivers to watch
Insurance	• Rate pricing and claims trends • Industry product growth • Product penetration • New products • Investment returns • Reserving and capital requirements • Regulatory changes
REGULATED	
Utilities	• Economic growth • Tariff changes • Utilization • Regulatory changes • Environmental concerns • Energy mix changes
Telecom	• Subscriber growth • ARPU changes • Regulatory changes • New entrants • Pricing • Technology cycle
CONGLOMERATES	
Conglomerates	• Refer to the specific business sections with similar earnings characteristics outlined in this table

SOURCE: Goldman Sachs Global Investment Research

Hyper Growth – Internet, Fintech, Biotechnology

Internet

The category currently known as the internet sector might disappear within a few years, as it contains more and more verticals with unique characteristics, such as advertising, social network services, e-commerce, delivery, entertainment, payment, education, car hailing, travel, property, and healthcare services, and it is increasingly difficult to refer to all of them in one category. What most businesses have in common though is the fact that an increase in online penetration is a core driver of their growth. So, the first important assumption an analyst will need to make is the online penetration rate of the vertical in 5 to 10 years. Then, down to a more granular level, detailed figures will need to be used to model earnings, such as gross merchandising value (GMV) growth, monthly active user (MAU) growth, average time spent on the app or site, take rate (the amount of revenue a company earns as commissions and charges versus GMV), and customer acquisition cost.

Given the relatively short history of the industry, official industry-level data is not widely available and analysts need to be mindful that the definitions of such data are often not consistent across companies. Another important point is profitability. Normally in traditional industries, dominant players enjoy higher profit margins due to pricing advantage and scale. But, in this high growth and 'winner-takes-all' type industry, profitability is often viewed as a trade-off relationship with its growth. Even the dominant top players sometimes need to control take rate and sacrifice margin in the pursuit of higher top-line growth. Regulatory pressures linked to data privacy and anti-monopoly concerns also weigh on the future profitability of dominant players in this industry, although the magnitude of the impact is still unclear.

Drivers to track include: 1) GMV growth, 2) MAU growth, 3) time spent on the app, 4) monetization rate, 5) advertising spend, 6) customer acquisition cost, and 7) regulatory changes.

Fintech

Financial technology (fintech) is becoming an important segment that needs to be discussed separately from the internet sector because of its significant potential market size and also the different regulatory environment it faces. Fintech business is broadly categorized into payment, lending, wealth management, and software solutions. Fintech companies basically aim to replace or supplement the traditional banking system through technology and higher mobile phone adoption, with the better-quality communication network having driven rapid growth in the past several years. Given the size of the potential TAM, the majority of large internet companies are currently focusing on this area. However, there also are a number of independent companies emerging with new business models. The profit model is similar to e-commerce with gross transaction value (GTV) multiplied by the take rate equating to the revenue. On the cost side are financing, credit provision, and R&D. Earnings models for companies that provide software solutions are similar to the ones used for software companies. It is perhaps useful to monitor various start-up companies providing technology solutions to make the internal processes of the financial industry more efficient by leveraging block chain technology. The difference between fintechs and other internet companies is that some fintech companies are regulated on their capital requirement and loan rate by regulators in the countries in which they operate. Changes in local regulations is something analysts need to watch carefully, as they can dramatically influence the outlook of the business.

Drivers to track include: 1) GTV growth, 2) MAU growth, 3) financing cost, 4) credit provision, 5) average lending rate, 6) customer acquisition cost, and 7) regulatory changes.

Biotechnology

In the biotechnology category, analysts are often asked to evaluate companies in the pre-revenue stage. Many biotech companies in their early stages only have a handful of drugs in the pipeline and thus understanding the development details of these individual drugs is critical. To forecast the potential revenue of a new drug, analysts will need to assess potential patient size of the targeted disease, all information on competing drugs globally, potential pricing, potential market shares, and the likely timing of approvals in various markets. Competition can come from small start-ups, global giants, or combinations of those, as seen in the Covid-19 vaccine development race in 2020. Even when evaluating the smaller start-up companies, an analyst will essentially need to map globally the whole drug development in the relevant areas. Connectivity with doctors, hospitals, and key opinion leaders (KOLs) is critical to gauge progress at the clinical stage. Because a company's value may be dependent on a few drugs, the trial data of relevant drugs, the announcement of new discoveries, and the approval of those drugs, could all alter a company's long-term earnings forecasts substantially. Therefore, analysts need to have a clear schedule of potential key announcements on both the company's own and also competitor's drugs, and interpret such data points in order to adjust the long-term earnings forecasts.

 Drivers to track include: 1) Potential TAM of the drug, 2) approval process of the drug, 3) clinical data of the drug, 4) news on competing drugs, 5) mergers and acquisitions in the relevant area, and 6) collaborations among key players.

Secular Growth – Software, Medical Technology

Software

The software industry is a key driver in the digital transformation of society, and the percentage of software, even within the overall IT spending market, has been consistently increasing, hence the industry enjoys long-term sustainable high growth. Adoption of subscription models such as software as a service (SaaS), platform as a service (PaaS), infrastructure as a service (IaaS), and public and private cloud services, have lowered the bar for new entrants as software providers, and those providers have subsequently expanded their customer base into smaller companies. Many highly specialized niche players are emerging and they tend to demonstrate very high top-line growth. Once they have built a relationship with a customer, many software companies tend to enjoy healthy pricing power. As they add more customers, operating leverage will be significant, given high upfront R&D costs, high customer acquisition costs, and high marginal profitability.

Monitoring the earnings trends of the software industry is not easy because of the limited industry data available, and analysts tend to rely on proprietary customer surveys. For large software companies, the pace of IT spending and spending patterns of major customer verticals, such as the finance, communication, consumer, and internet industries, is something analysts should be closely monitoring. For smaller companies, specific customer wins and competitive dynamics of those particular segments, are important to follow.

 Drivers to track include: 1) IT spending growth, 2) growth of the client's industry revenue pool, 3) client wins, 4) market share changes, 5) outsourcing trend of customers, 6) regulatory changes, and 7) new business models.

Medical Technology

The medical technology industry has a very wide range of sub-segments such as cardiology, orthopaedics, surgery, dental, diabetes, eye health, dialysis, neuromodulation, radiation oncology, and supplies. Innovations in this industry are accelerating, driven by the advancement of enabling technologies such as imaging, sensors, control, materials, software, artificial intelligence (AI), 3D printing, and augmented reality. Medical technology is generally resilient against economic cycles and typically enjoys a fairly stable pricing environment due to high technology barriers and switching costs, offset by reimbursement limitations and customer leverage.

Earnings should be driven by the number of surgeries (ageing population), the hospital capex cycle, and a company's new product cycle. Currently, particularly notable growth areas include robotics surgery, minimally invasive cardiology categories, sensors such as continuous glucose monitors, vision care, and other minimally invasive procedures. Emerging market penetration is another source of growth for medical device companies. New product approvals from regulators are one of the key events analysts need to watch. Large-scale litigation could also potentially be a risk.

 Drivers to track include: 1) volume of patients, 2) volume of surgeries, 3) hospital capacity, 4) clinical data, 5) approval of new products, 5) regulatory changes, and 6) hospital capex budget.

Cyclical – Capital Goods, Transport, Energy, Commodities, Chemicals, Autos

Capital Goods

Earnings of capital goods companies, such as machine tools, automation equipment, construction machinery, large vessel, rolling stock, mining equipment, and various other types of manufacturing equipment, are very cyclical. The earnings typically move in parallel with economic activities, such as industrial production. When the underlying industry environment is good, the demand for capital goods goes up substantially as many users of such products increase capacity. If the environment is weak, they stop buying equipment. Such equipment typically has a replacement cycle of 5 to 10 years and the industry normally alternates multi-year upcycle and down-cycle. So, if a company or third-party is forecasting more than five years of consecutive upturns or downturns for this industry, an analyst should question this. Factors such as tougher environmental regulations can sometimes accelerate the replacement cycle. Also, some segments of capital goods are considered as early cycle and some are late cycle depending on the nature of the products.

 Drivers to track include: 1) demand in clients' industries, 2) economic cycle, such as industrial production, 3) replacement cycle, and 4) environmental regulation.

Transport

The transport industry segment includes shipping, railways, and airlines. Earnings of the companies are typically driven by the volume of traffic, fleet capacity, unit service price, and fuel price. Earnings can be highly volatile given the high fixed cost nature of the business, while short-term fluctuation of unit service prices, such as ticket prices and fleet charges, further amplify the volatility. Changes in fuel cost also add more fluctuations in profitability. Earnings cyclicality for companies in the transport sector tends to be more short term than for capital goods companies, as the former can carry high financial leverage due to heavy capital investment. Changes in financing costs are also something analysts need to watch with care.

 Drivers to track include: 1) passenger traffic, 2) fleet capacity, 3) fuel price, 4) cargo demand, and 5) cost of financing.

Energy

The biggest driver of earnings for energy-related companies is the price of crude oil price and liquefied natural gas (LNG). Energy companies often own assets in different layers, such as upstream exploration, refinery, pipeline, downstream chemical, and distribution. If the company has upstream assets, the progress of exploration projects can be a significant earnings swing factor. If it has refinery assets, refining margins have their own demand and supply dynamics, which are not necessarily always correlated with oil price. The energy distribution business could be influenced by policy changes of local governments. Given the significant size of the energy sector, the oil and gas service sector, which provides various support for the exploration process, is also a significant sub-sector. The business of this sub-sector is dependent on the capex cycle of oil and gas companies, hence the earnings tend to move in parallel, similar to the pattern seen in the capital goods sector.

 Drivers to track include: 1) crude oil price, 2) progress of exploration projects, 3) refiner demand and supply, and 4) capex cycle.

Commodities

Underlying demand and supply of the product is the most important earnings driver of the base metals industry such as steel, copper, and aluminium. Understanding the real picture of global industry supply is not a straightforward exercise, as companies do not always fully disclose production levels. Raw material costs and energy costs, such as iron ore price and coking coal price, are also important to the earnings but such prices are easy to follow. Given the wide usage of these products, the relevant cycle generally moves in conjunction with industry production.

 Drivers to track include: 1) underlying product demand and supply, 2) product inventories, 3) demand and supply of middle products and by-products, and 4) disruption in mining operations, and 5) changes in raw material costs.

Chemicals

Earnings drivers of the chemical industry are similar to those for metal industry. Upstream commodity chemical products tend to be driven more by the broader macro environment and industry level demand and supply. The petrochemical segment has five manufacturing chains: olefins (ethylene, propylene); vinyl (polyvinyl chloride (PVC), caustic soda); rubber (synthetic rubber, latex); benzene (styrene, acrylonitrile-butadiene-styrene (ABS)); and polyester (polyethylene terephthalate (PET)), and each chain tends to have slightly different demand and supply dynamics.

A quarterly level of detailed demand-and-supply analysis is critical in production of an accurate earnings forecasts for this industry. Downstream speciality chemical products are more influenced by the demand of specific end products, such as household goods, autos, semiconductors, and displays. A sudden supply shortage of such products, e.g. due to a production halt by a major manufacturer, could cause a sharp price hike. It would have a positive impact on the earnings of other manufacturers in the same product category but would be very negative if such a price hike happened to their feed stock. It is important to consistently monitor 'real' global supply capacities of the products, as the total of published capacities is not always the actual functioning capacity.

 Drivers to track include: 1) end product demand, 2) price of feed stock, 3) product pricing, 4) production capacity expansion and utilization, 5) demand and supply of each manufacturing chain, and 6) inventory level.

Autos

Demand for autos is generally driven by consumer sentiment, fuel prices, and interest rates. These factors not only impact the volume of vehicles sold but also the mix of vehicle sales. When oil prices go down, larger cars with lower fuel economy tend to sell well. Higher interest rates are generally negative for car demand as most people buy cars with loans. Changes in emission regulations of each country can drive replacement cycles. Given the global nature of the industry, currency rates also influence earnings. Some emerging countries provide government subsidies for car purchases in order to stimulate their economies.

At an individual company level, the model change cycle is an important factor. Companies that launch successful new models tend to gain market share for that year. Most major car manufacturers sell into global markets and have manufacturing sites in different countries, so currency fluctuations can have a large impact on their earnings. The emergence of electric vehicles (EVs) adds new complexity to the earnings structure of car companies. Currently, most car makers lose money on EVs because of high battery costs and development cost burden. However, the continuous cost reduction of batteries and government subsidies for electric vehicle purchases could make the business profitable in the future.

 Drivers to track include: 1) new model cycle, 2) gas prices, 3) consumer sentiment, 4) interest rates, 5) currency fluctuations, and 6) emission regulation changes.

Cyclical Growth – Semiconductor, Electronic Components, Technology Hardware, Clean Energy

Semiconductor

The semiconductor industry is another key driver of technological advancement. Almost every year, faster processing power and larger memory capacity with lower cost is offered thanks to shrinking line width and other advanced process technologies. As such, both demand and supply, meaning demand of chips both in terms of speed and transistor density and its production volume, are currently growing at a rather high pace year-on-year. Semiconductor companies need enormous capital expenditure and R&D budgets every year to keep up with the technology progress and volume needs. Memory devices (which store data) such as DRAM and NAND are standardized products and prices have a tendency towards large swings in price depending on the prevailing demand and supply situation. The memory market is dominated by three to four large global players. Logic devices (which compute data), such as the CPU and graphics processing unit (GPU), are more specialized but are increasingly designed by fabless companies and manufactured by foundries. As many logic products are designed for specific end products, price volatility tends to be lower than for memory devices.

Semiconductor production equipment (SPE) is also a large industry and drives a core part of process technology innovation. SPE revenue is even more volatile than memory given the nature of being capital goods, although this is mostly due to volume fluctuation rather than price changes. Drivers of the semiconductor cycle include a major technology shift of end market products, such as the new generation smartphone launch, and the economic situation. At the company level, medium-term market share shifts are also an important factor when forecasting earnings trends, although the competitive dynamics do not change quickly. Over time, the speed at which China could catch up with the United States and Japan on high-end technology could change the industry landscape considerably.

 Drivers to track include: 1) memory price cycle, 2) capex cycle, 3) end product demand outlook, 4) product substitution, 5) process technology migration, and 6) market share changes within category.

Electronic Components

The electronic components industry includes a wide range of categories. Some require sophisticated process technology, such as LCD, organic light-emitting diode (OLED), and multi-layer ceramic capacitors (MLCC). These components share similar earnings characteristics to semiconductors because they enjoy constant efficiency gains through process migration, they face constant price pressure from the end products at the same time, and they are capital intensive. Earnings of mechanical parts, such as motors, lenses, sensors, and actuators are mostly driven by end-product launch timing, product demand, inventory, and pricing power of the component companies. In this latter segment, market share shifts due to design win or loss happen relatively frequently and it is important for analysts to follow the monthly level revenue trends.

 Drivers to track include: 1) end product demand outlook, 2) customer wins and losses, 3) inventory level, and 4) product substitution.

Technology Hardware (Enterprise)

A large segment of enterprise hardware is communication equipment, such as base stations, switches, and routers. Earnings for these companies are driven largely by the capex of telecom carriers. The capex cycle they face is less influenced by the economy and instead mainly by the industry-wide global technology migrations that occur every few years, such as 4G and 5G technology. Other major enterprise technology, such as servers and storage devices are primarily driven by the IT spending of large corporations. As the outsourcing trend of cloud services prevails, a handful of large-scale cloud service companies will share a larger portion of such capex, hence the earnings trend of enterprise hardware businesses will start to depend more on the company-specific capex cycles. Given the global nature of the industry, currency moves are something to be monitored as well.

 Drivers to track include: 1) customer spending, 2) technology migration, 3) product cycle, 4) customer wins and losses, and 5) currency fluctuations.

Technology Hardware (Consumer)

The main products in the consumer technology industry have been changing over time. This segment used to be dominated by PC-related products, but now the main product is smartphones. The next major products could be wearable devices, such as smart watches, advanced earphones, smart glasses, and virtual reality (VR) devices. In every cycle it is difficult to know exactly what will be the 'next big thing' but in the past 50 years the next big thing has always come and driven the industry growth.

The biggest earnings driver of this segment is the product cycle. Product market share moves rather frequently depending on consumer tastes, and the whole supply chain is then affected by it. Given the nature of these consumer technology products, demand is highly seasonal with the December quarter and Christmas season traditionally sharing a large portion of the annual revenue. In recent years, the market in China has been adding extra cycles to the global demand for consumer technology products due to their own holiday seasons (Chinese New Year, National Day Golden Week, etc.). The cost of components, such as DRAM, NAND, MLCC, and LCD, and also currency rates can influence the profitability of the products.

 Drivers to track include: 1) new product cycle, 2) product pricing, 3) market share changes, 4) component costs, and 5) currency fluctuations.

Clean Energy

The main products of the clean energy segment are solar panels, electric vehicle batteries, wind turbines, smart grid equipment, and the components that go into those products. Given the social and political pressure to decarbonize society, the potential growth opportunities of those markets are significant. Products such as solar panels have become cost competitive against traditional energy sources in certain countries with consistent sunlight, and hence no longer require subsidies. Electric vehicle batteries still need substantial cost reductions to compete against internal combustion engines. In any case, to capture the large demand, makers of those products need to achieve constant cost reductions. As technology barriers of those products are typically not very high, the potential for industry oversupply due to new entrants is something analysts need to monitor carefully. Any policy change from governments could have a strong influence on earnings for clean energy companies. Lower oil prices have historically led to a slowdown in clean energy capex, but given carbon neutral pledges by various countries globally over the past few years, this impact will become less significant going forward.

 Drivers to track include: 1) capex, 2) unit price reduction, 3) demand and supply, 4) energy price, 5) policy changes, and 6) large new project launches.

Stable – Consumer Staples, Retail, Consumer Discretionary, Pharmaceutical, Media, Business Services

Consumer Staples

By its definition the demand for consumer staples products, such as food, beverages, and household goods, are less sensitive to the economic cycle. Market growth of such products are limited in most developed countries. As such, companies in this category try to grow their earnings through product upgrades, new product additions, geographic expansion, and mergers and acquisitions (M&A). Hence, analysts need to monitor the market share trend of each product closely and try to understand why markets shares are moving in a certain direction. On top of market share data prepared by data research companies, real time stock keeping unit (SKU) and pricing data available on the internet can sometimes offer useful insights. Weather can also be an important demand swing factor for some products such as beer and soft drinks. For the longer-term outlook, increasing health consciousness, the emergence of niche brands driven by social network service (SNS), and consumption upgrade in emerging countries, are all important underlying trends.

 Drivers to track include: 1) consumption trend, 2) channel shift, 3) market share, 4) product pricing, and 5) weather.

Retail

Earnings of retailing companies are primarily driven by the pace of store openings and revenue growth of existing stores (same store growth). Same store growth is driven by consumer behaviour and competitive dynamics. Close monitoring of monthly same store growth data of each company and analysis of trend changes will be important. The gross margins of retailing companies are relatively stable but changes in labour costs and rents can affect profitability. Competition from online companies is the most significant challenge facing this industry and the medium-term earnings outlook is largely influenced by the level of resiliency against the threat of online competition. Convenience stores and speciality stores are relatively resilient but undifferentiated general merchandising stores are more vulnerable. A current interesting debate is how much fresh grocery products can increase online penetration. Some retailers are making efforts to enhance their own online businesses and some are partnering with online players or being acquired by them.

Drivers to track include: 1) store openings, 2) same store revenue growth, 3) increase in private label products, 4) competition from online, 5) development of new formats, 6) labour cost, and 7) rental cost.

Consumer Discretionary

Earnings of the consumer discretionary segment, including furniture, white goods, luxury goods, apparel, leisure, restaurants, and entertainment, are largely driven by the economic cycle. As consumers buy those products or services when discretionary income is higher, the earnings are more pro-cyclical than other consumer-related products. At the individual company level, new product cycle and market share changes are important drivers of earnings. Demand for furniture and white goods is also influenced by housing starts. Weather or temperature is also an important demand factor for some sectors such as apparel, leisure, and entertainment. Although analysts are unlikely to be able to accurately forecast the weather, they do need to understand past weather patterns when analysing year over year trends on monthly revenues. Emerging market demand is a very important growth driver for certain segments such as luxury goods, white goods, and apparel.

Drivers to track include: 1) product cycle, 2) demand cycle driven by the economy, 3) market share changes, 4) weather, and 5) emerging market demand growth.

Pharmaceutical

Earnings of pharmaceutical companies are mainly driven by the sales of major drugs, which should not fluctuate in the short term. Earnings drivers can come in the form of new drug approvals, drug reimbursement price changes, and the emergence of competing drugs. When patents on a company's drugs expire, it tends to lose market share because low-cost generic drugs will start to emerge. Various costs associated with legal disputes can also influence earnings. To forecast the long-term earnings, analysts need to have a large database that contains long-term forecasts of major drugs globally, and to constantly update this when a new development occurs in the competitive landscape. In most cases such revisions are subtle ones for large companies but occasionally one clinical data release or an announcement of a new discovery can have a significant impact on future earnings. Anticipating such announcements and preparing for the potential earnings impact are important events for an analyst to deal with.

 Drivers to track include: 1) changes in TAM of major drugs, 2) new drug approval process, 3) M&A activities in the relevant areas, and 4) healthcare policies.

Media

Earnings of media companies, such as TV, cable TV, satellite TV, radio, music label, and publishers, are largely driven by advertising revenue, subscription numbers, and the cost of content production or acquisition. Advertising budget generally moves in-line with the profitability of large advertisers, such as autos, household goods, and food and beverage. Subscription numbers are normally stable through the economic cycle but similar to the situation in the retail industry, 'traditional media' companies are subject to the threat from online entertainment companies. Increasingly, more traditional TV companies are starting their own subscription video on demand (SVOD) to defend the TAM from growing online players and because the content acquisition cost can weigh on profitability. Some large content owners have also started to distribute their content directly to consumers.

 Drivers to track include: 1) consumer sentiment, 2) profitability of consumer companies, 3) content acquisition costs, and 4) competition from online.

Business Services

The business services sector encompasses a wide range of areas, including staffing, office administration, logistics, catering, cleaning, and security. These services essentially allow client companies to outsource non-core operations, reduce fixed costs, and to focus on the core competences. Although it is difficult to generalize the whole area, the outsourcing trend of corporates is a key driver of industry growth and earnings tend to be defensive to economic cycles. As corporates generally outsource parts of businesses that are difficult to differentiate, such businesses tend to be labour intensive and with lower entry barriers. As such, the success of the business services industry depends on the scale and execution.

 Drivers to track include: 1) business trend of clients' industry, 2) outsourcing trend, 3) competition, and 4) cost inflation.

Interest Rate Sensitive – REITs, Property Developers, Banks, Insurance

REITs

Real estate investment trusts (REITs), companies that own income-producing real estate across a range of property sectors, act like a fixed income instrument with investors expecting a certain level of stable cash dividends. They basically pay out 100% (or sometimes more) of net profit. Many REITs acquire assets from their sponsors to grow the business and they also normally raise equity to finance those acquisitions. Analysts need to monitor the cash flow generation ability of the underlying assets, including occupancy rate and rental rate revisions. Each REIT has a different mix of assets, such as office buildings, residential buildings, retail assets, industrial assets, and hospitals, with each facing a slightly different cycle. Although business performance should have some correlation with the economic cycle, REIT earnings tend not to be very volatile because rental contracts are generally multi-year. Logistics REITs and data centre REITs are relatively new growth areas in this sector. Financing cost is also an important factor to consider when looking at earnings.

 Drivers to track include: 1) occupancy rate of underlying assets, 2) change in rental charges, 3) asset acquisitions, 4) change in financing cost, and 5) government policy.

Property Developers

The property development sector includes developer business and landlord business. Landlord business is a stable recurring income business and analysts need to monitor occupancy rates and rents.

In contrast, the property development business can be quite variable, as it records large profits when projects are completed. The availability of funding is key for the property development business and hence it becomes more active when interest rates are lower. In some countries like China, housing policies can be used to help control economic growth. In such cases, analysts need to watch the government's direction of lending control closely.

 Drivers to track include: 1) unit sales, 2) unit pricing, 3) changes in cap rate, 4) landbank acquisition, 5) occupancy rate, 6) dividend pay-out, 7) financing cost, and 8) government policy.

Banks

Banks' earnings are generally tied to the macroeconomic climate of the geographic areas, interest rate cycles, and companies they are most exposed to. The majority of the revenue for a bank comes from net interest income, or the spread between the interest its customers pay to the bank on loans and the cost of funding it pays out to fund the balance sheet. Banks may also sell other financial products (insurance, asset management, wealth management and so forth) and the associated fees form the core of non-interest income growth. The largest driver of cyclical change is bad debts, or how well credit quality weathers economic cycles. Banks are deemed pro-cyclical for this reason, as they reflect the cyclical nature of the business cycle and also given the limited capital relative to the size of the balance sheet. So, a small change in asset quality can quickly produce losses and if large enough it can test the capital level. It is also important to pay attention to penetration of these financial products in an economy, and the loan growth rates relative to the underlying growth rates of the economy. Lastly, analysts should remember that the relationship between the balance sheet and income statement is inseparable, as governments determine required levels of capital and reserving. Regulatory changes to these required levels can have a significant impact on the ability of a bank to grow its loan book and interest income. The levered nature of banks also adds to the pro-cyclicality.

 Drivers to track include: 1) industry data on loans and deposits, 2) interest rates, 3) capital levels, 4) liquidity management (loan and deposit ratios), 5) interest rate risk management, duration, and rate sensitivity, 6) asset quality indicators and credit risk management, and 7) regulatory changes.

Insurance

Insurance is the protection against future risk of an event in return for a current premium and the sector is divided into life insurance and property and casualty (fire, auto, house, etc.). The insurance underwriting cycle is generally also cyclical, largely as a function of the capital the industry currently holds, albeit more stable than the same metric for banks. Earnings growth starts as a function of the growth rates of the underlying assets in the economy that are being insured and the penetration of these products. Many emerging markets are still at the nascent stages of penetration. Products may also be structured very differently and analysts should pay particular attention to these structures to understand what the revenue drivers may be. For example, if these products have savings and investment components in them, it will be necessary to understand the economics of these insurance floats (the gap between the premium collected and claims paid out), in terms of duration, profit share, etc., to accurately calibrate the insurer's earnings. The balance sheet and capital levels are typically highly regulated, and it will be important for analysts to speak to actuaries or other experts to understand the dynamics of reserving and capital requirements, and how a change in product suites may impact these.

Drivers to track include: 1) rate pricing and claims trends, 2) industry product growth, 3) product penetration, 4) new products, 5) investment returns, 6) reserving and capital requirements, and 7) regulatory changes.

Regulated – Utilities, Telecoms

Utilities

Earnings of utilities companies, such as electricity power generators, power distributors and gas distributors, are driven by power demand, tariff changes, and changes in input costs. In many cases the business may be a monopoly and heavily regulated by the government. Tariffs are largely determined by a formula based on the prevailing regulation, and volumes are driven by economic activity and weather patterns. The cost side tends to be volatile as input costs, such as coal, gas, and oil, fluctuate. As nuclear power plants tend to have lower generation costs, suspension of nuclear capacity will be negative to the overall profitability of a power company. Given the mounting pressure globally on CO_2 reduction, power companies are increasing their investment in wind and solar power capacity, which will change their profit structure going forward.

Drivers to track include: 1) economic growth, 2) tariff changes, 3) utilization, 4) regulatory changes, 5) environmental concerns, and 6) energy mix changes.

Telecoms

The major earnings drivers of the telecommunication sector are subscriber growth and average revenue per user (ARPU) growth. In most developed countries, mobile subscribers are saturated and ARPU is under pressure. Technology migration, such as 5G in the next few years, provides opportunities for telecom carriers to increase ARPU through a higher performance service. But the ability to hike prices is not straightforward as mobile phone tariffs often become a political agenda because it is very visible within people's disposable income. As seen in some countries like India, spectrum auctions to acquire the capacity can create a substantial burden on telecom companies' future cash flow. Additionally, new entrants to the market will put further pressure on ARPU, as seen in both India and Japan recently. Given the challenging environment facing their core business, telecom companies are mainly seeking growth through two areas. One area is entertainment and media services to consumers, leveraging enormous customer connectivity. The other is value-added communication infrastructure services to corporate customers by leveraging the significant infrastructure to their advantage. However, at this stage, it is not clear if those new areas can drive earnings substantially in the future.

 Drivers to track include: 1) subscriber growth, 2) ARPU changes, 3) regulatory changes, 4) new entrants, 5) pricing, and 6) technology cycle.

Conglomerates

Conglomerate companies generally fall into one of two types: 1) companies with a large number of business lines that are directly operated under one corporate entity, and 2) investment companies with multiple independent assets. The former type globally has increasingly been divesting 'non-core' business lines, and pursuing synergies among 'core' business lines to reduce application of a conglomerate discount (as discussed in Chapter 6 on valuation). Some of the latter type of companies provide value to shareholders through strong track records of divesting and acquiring assets at the right time. In either case, although time consuming, analysts need to treat and analyse individual assets like independent companies. As the level of disclosure might be lower for individual businesses, collaboration with sector specialists is particularly important. Given the complexity, analysing such individual businesses can potentially offer interesting value discovery opportunities that the market may have overlooked.

 Drivers to track: To understand the earnings drivers of the individual businesses of conglomerates, please refer to the specific business sections with similar earnings characteristics discussed earlier in this chapter.

Where to
start

What to
avoid

Understand the unique ✔
earnings characteristics of
the industry

✘ Forgetting about macro
trends

Know the specific earn- ✔
ings drivers of the industry

✘ Being behind the curve
in realizing the structural
changes of the earnings
drivers

Identify the appropriate
statistics to monitor the ✔
earnings drivers

✘ Discounting the impor-
tance of regulatory risks

Understand earnings sensi- ✔
tivity to different factors

SOURCE: Goldman Sachs Global Investment Research

Chapter 3
Identify the 'Personality' of the Company

Once an analyst has researched the industry, the next area of focus is learning about the qualitative side of the company. The goal of this process is to identify the 'personality' of the company: who they are, what they do, how they make money, how they grow, etc. This is the equivalent of the equity story for an Initial Public Offering (IPO) company. By digging deeper, it should be possible to find nuanced information that simple financial statements cannot express. The 'personality' of a company can change over time, which can drive the value of a company down or up. This is potentially one of the most interesting parts of the company analysis process for analysts.

Product and Service

Studying the industry should have included extensive research on products and services from the industry perspective. The next step is to learn about these at a company specific level, with a particular focus on the strengths and weaknessess versus competing products and services. This is especially the case when dealing with industrial goods, where detailed comparisons versus competitors on mechanical structure, manufacturing process, raw materials, unit price, level of customers, etc., are all very important as they provide the basis for thinking about competitive moat and profitability. If the company provides a service to consumers, analysts need to step back and identify the underlying value proposition of that service from a consumer's point of view, as opposed to what the company says it aims to provide.

Origin and History

While it is easy to jump into the current status of the company and look forward, it is equally important to step back and study the history of the company, as this often gives an analyst a better understanding of the DNA of the company. For example, Company A and Company B are currently very similar, producing and selling the same products. But Company A started as a distributor of the product and went upstream, while Company B started life as a research laboratory designing the technology and then became a manufacturer. There is a good chance their decision making would be different in terms of diversification, geographic expansion, new product development, acquisitions, etc. Using another example, Company C and Company D had a similar level of technology in a certain high-tech product but Company C originated in a small country with a limited local market and Company D originated in a large country with a lucrative local market. As the market of the product globalized, Company C was better in gaining a global market share than did Company D as the latter had always targeted the global market. There are many other aspects of corporate history that can be examined to aid a deeper understanding of the company, such as the level of competition, business mix changes, bargaining power with customers, and management transitions.

Management Profile

It may be stating the obvious, but the personality, capability, and track record of a CEO can have a tremendous impact on a company's strategy, culture, and performance. When analysing a company, analysts should spend a significant amount of time studying the CEO's profile. If they have written books/articles or have given published interviews then those are a good place to start understanding them better, including non-work-related activities. The senior management of other companies in the industry could also provide a pretty good sense of the strengths and weaknesses of the management team being researched. Multiple sources should be sought and reviewed to reduce any bias. In cases where direct access to the CEO is a possibility, spend time on their long-term vision and ambition. Although business plans can be read on paper, you really only get a true sense of his or her vision and ambition when meeting them in person. Don't waste valuable time with CEOs on detailed questions that an Investor Relations manager can answer another time. Meeting with key senior management as well, such as the Chief Financial Officer (CFO) and also division heads, aids in gauging the depth of management capability.

Ownership Structure

A great deal of the character of a company will be defined by who owns and controls it. Ownership by founders, governments, families, private equity, group ownership, activists, or a circular structure each provide different incentives to company management.

Although it is risky to stereotype the character of a company based purely on the shareholding, a proper understanding of the shareholders is an important part of company analysis. This is especially the case when finding large less well-known shareholders, and analysts need to make a really good effort to understand their designations. Complicated ownership structures, like those seen in the Korean chaebol (large corporate group) companies, have the potential to weigh on a company's valuation.

Value Chain

When digging deeper into analysing a company, especially when comparing it with industry peers, it starts to become clear which parts of value chain the company really excels at. Not many companies do everything perfectly, but successful companies definitely do something really well. It is very useful to identify which parts of the value chain, such as product innovation, product quality, customer service, brand power, patent, channel management, manufacturing cost, raw material sourcing, logistics, provide the company's real competitive advantage.

Suppose there are two consumer electronics companies, Company A that consistently launches innovative products with sleek designs and Company B whose products are of good quality but not quite so innovative and a bit boring. From a consumer point of view one might assume Company A would do better. But in reality, the financial performance of Company B is more consistent thanks to its extensive distribution channel and better inventory control system. Although this is not something that can be learnt by just looking at income statements, a thorough analysis of peer group companies and extensive discussions with industry experts should give analysts some ideas. One possible approach is to compare the cash return on capital invested (CROCI) breakdown with industry peers, in terms of asset turnover, profit margin, and cash conversion. Why these metrics may be higher or lower than peers can provide a good starting point for the analysis. CROCI is discussed in more detail in Chapter 6 on valuation.

Some companies refer to an 'asset light business model' as being to their advantage, but such claims can only be valid when a company outsources part of the value chain where it is not competitive and instead concentrates its efforts on other parts of value chain where it can excel against competitors. Simply not owning a part of the value chain does not make a company more efficient and better than peers.

Competitive Moat

One of the most important aspects of any company analysis is to identify the competitive moat. Having a top market-share position is an effect not a cause. Analysts need to understand why the company has this market share. The distinction has to be made between a company that was in the right place at the right time for a short period, and a company with a sustainable competitive moat. As mentioned in the value chain discussion, each company has its strengths and weaknesses. The question is whether these strengths are enough to create a sustainable competitive moat for the company. The most visible and obvious competitive moats are brand, patent, and platform. It takes a long time to build a strong brand, platform, or solid patent portfolio, and it is expensive to acquire them. Hence, luxury brands, pharmaceutical companies (patents), semiconductor foundries (platforms), and e-commerce platforms can enjoy sustainable high margins.

Switching costs can also be a strong competitive moat. High-tech business-to-business (B2B) areas, such as semiconductor production equipment, medical equipment, or enterprise software, have a high switching cost for users and it is difficult to gain share from the top companies. Industry leading scale, such as production volume, store numbers, and user numbers, can be a competitive moat but it is more important to understand why they gained such a scale. If they achieved the leading share just by being early, their current positions might be vulnerable. Geographic positioning and country regulations can be a competitive moat as well. Given its remote geographic location and relatively low population density, penetration of retail industries in Australia by global online retailers has happened at a slower pace compared with other developed countries. When the government in China placed restrictions on global internet companies coming into the country, this greatly helped local internet players. There are subtler competitive moats, such as ability to innovate, creative marketing, strong channel relationships, and tight execution; it requires more effort to understand how strong those moats are.

Track Record of Strategic Decisions

Reviewing a company's past key strategic decisions is also a useful exercise for an analyst. How aggressively did it expand the business through capex, advertising spending, or acquisitions, when market opportunities were identified? In order to grow, did the company diversify to new areas extensively or strengthen its core areas to gain market share? Did the company retreat from a new project quickly enough after realizing it would fail? Did the company take a larger risk in development to be a technology leader or focus on trailing edge products to capture more secure profitability? Those characteristics of a company's decision-making are unlikely to change in the short term, hence it can be assumed that it will take a similar strategic path in the future.

Corporate Culture by Country

It is too simplistic to characterize companies based on the location of their headquarters, but there are some broad trends related to corporate culture in each region that are useful to understand when looking at the corporate strategy element. This is something that can be learnt through experience. US companies have a keen focus on capital efficiencies and shareholder return. European companies tend to be balanced to all the stakeholders. Chinese companies tend to be quick in decision-making and do not hesitate to try new things. Japanese companies are often obsessed with product quality and can be relatively slow in decision-making. Korean companies tend to set high goals and are willing to make drastic changes. The point here is not to have prejudice on these ideals but to see companies within the context of the broader corporate culture. It is a well-known story that Korean semiconductor memory companies gained a substantial market share in the 1990s by making large contrarian capex during the industry downturn, while Japanese companies did not take such a risk and thus lost market share. The differences in corporate cultures possibly played a significant role in this.

Earnings Guidance Track Record

It is possible to learn something about a company from the way it forecasts its own earnings and guides the market. For the purposes of understanding the personality of the company, continuous earnings misses can often be a sign of weak execution and cost management. Tight earnings forecasts with clean explanations could be a sign of high-quality planning and execution of the business. Each industry has differing levels of earnings predictability, but well-run companies do tend to manage earnings expectations better than their peers.

Controversy Record

A company's history of controversies, such as litigation, accidents, employee disputes, and regulatory breaches will need to be checked. If there are some pending cases, analysts may need to seek advice from legal experts to ensure they fully understand the issues. There have been plenty of examples of an accounting cover up or an employee-related issue then catalysing larger issues that result in threats to a company's existence as a publicly traded company. So, if analysts find controversies related to a company during their research process, it is advisable to raise them for discussion with internal research management (i.e. during an Investment Review Committee meeting) as potential red flags.

Management Quality – A Framework

Assessing management quality is the most important, and the most difficult, part of company analysis because it is a subjective concept and tough to quantify. A checklist like that shown in Figure 3.1 is useful when analysts are thinking about the quality of company management. Although this list may be broader than ones normally used when assessing management quality criteria, it is important to look at this factor holistically. The aim of the framework is not necessarily to score each item and come up with total scores. It can be used instead to understand and compare management quality with those of industry peers. Some company managements are very well rounded and do not appear to lack anything on the list. Some are strong in one or two areas but relatively weak in the rest. It would be quite interesting for an analyst to identify whether the differences have manifested themselves in the company's financial performance.

Figure 3.1   Sample management scorecard

STRATEGY: Does the company have a compelling strategy?

Clear target business domains	✔
Differentiation versus competitors	✘
Forward vision	✔
Ambition	✘
Willingness to adapt to changes	✘

RESOURCING: Does the company have sufficient resources to succeed?

Technology – patents, R&D capability	✔
Franchise – customers, distributors, suppliers	✘
Depth of talent pool	✔
Funding	✘

EXECUTION: Does the company have the ability to execute the strategy?

Numerical targets	✔
Execution timeline	✘
Key performance indicators (KPIs) for management	✔
Proper incentive scheme	✘
Cost discipline	✘
Speed	✔

INTEGRITY: Can investors trust the company?

Compliance track record	✔
Environmental and social engagement	✘
Reputation with suppliers	✔
Governance structure	✘
Speed to correct mistakes	✘

SHAREHOLDER ORIENTATION: Does the company align its interests with shareholders?

Communication with investors	✔
Management ownership	✘
Share buyback policy	✔
Dividend policy	✘
History of value-destroying decisions	✘

SOURCE: Goldman Sachs Global Investment Research

Where to **start**

What to **avoid**

Focus on the qualitative aspects of the company

 Looking ahead without looking back – don't skip the history

Figure out which part of the value chain the company can really add value to

Just believing a company's story without critical eyes

Understand the DNA of the company

Viewing products and services from the perspective of the company rather than the consumer

Identify the competitive moat

Overlooking cultural and regional nuances

Asking the CEO about the next quarter

SOURCE: Goldman Sachs Global Investment Research

AUTHOR ANECDOTE

Recently I met the Chairman of a leading Japanese company in the semiconductor industry that I used to cover. The company has done phenomenally well both operationally and financially in the past 10 plus years since I stopped covering them. Granted that they were in a good industry, the company's performance has been outstanding against peers. I casually asked him why he thought they did so well and his answer was that they listened well to the advice from the capital market and implemented it. I was pleasantly shocked he quoted that as the first reason. Twenty years ago, when I started to cover this company, although it was already one of the leading companies in terms of market share, the financial performance was volatile. Given the highly cyclical nature of its product demand and the long production lead time, the cash flow management was poor. Also, the profit margin was lower than their US peers. I had a number of conversations with the top management, including the Chairman, pointing out those issues, and consequently the company made persistent efforts to improve cash flow management and operating efficiency.

As an analyst, I had a number of similar conversations with their peers but very few took the feedback so seriously. I am under no illusion that I was the only one suggesting those issues to the company. It is also arrogant to believe people in the financial industry know how to manage a technology company better than their management. However, occasionally,

(Continued)

AUTHOR ANECDOTE (*Continued*)

there are some situations that capital market professionals can see the 'blind spot' of a company and make suggestions to improve its performance. Although it is not a main function of the equity analyst, they are in the unique position of being able to establish unbiased relationships with top management and potentially influence strategies of the company within the boundary of compliance rules. Such trusted relationships could add depth and joy to the career of an analyst, at least it did to mine.

Part III

Analyse and
Apply the Findings

Chapter 4
Put Findings into the Earnings Model

The next step for an analyst is to put all the knowledge and insights accumulated so far into a company's earnings model (see Figure 4.1). Basic earnings models should include a segmental breakdown, income statement, balance sheet, and cash flow statement, and the four sheets should be connected to each other. Ideally once an analyst has built the model and is used to it, they can undertake simulations in their heads. A good earnings model understands what the most important assumptions are and is built so that these assumptions can be flexed to see the impact on bottom line profit and fair value. It should also be easy to update and manipulate. The importance of historical data should not be overlooked. Thorough analysis of 10 to 20 years of financial data can tell analysts a lot about a company. Earnings models can be used not only to help analysts forecast future earnings but also to help them understand a company better. While the model will focus on one company, analysts should compare the figures against similar companies in the same industry and think about why certain values are

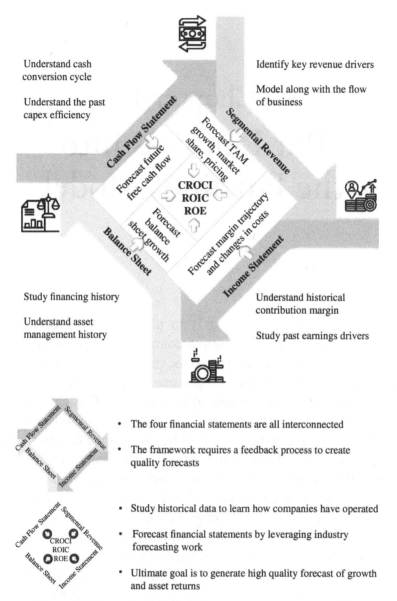

Understand cash conversion cycle

Understand the past capex efficiency

Identify key revenue drivers

Model along with the flow of business

Study financing history

Understand asset management history

Understand historical contribution margin

Study past earnings drivers

- The four financial statements are all interconnected

- The framework requires a feedback process to create quality forecasts

- Study historical data to learn how companies have operated

- Forecast financial statements by leveraging industry forecasting work

- Ultimate goal is to generate high quality forecast of growth and asset returns

Figure 4.1 Framework for building company earnings models

SOURCE: Goldman Sachs Global Investment Research

different to others' figures. In this chapter, a regular manufacturing company is used as the example and comments specific to other industries are then discussed.

Segmental Revenue Forecast

The segmental breakdown in a financial model has a free format, allowing analysts to show creativity and differentiation. Well-constructed information by segment can give a very good idea of how the company operates, makes money, and grows. Analysts should start by using the industry growth forecasts and market share assumptions, split by sub-segment, as discussed in Chapter 1. The earnings drivers discussed in Chapter 2 should then drive the flow of the model. Companies normally provide segmental information in their disclosures but an analyst's model should go into significantly more detail. Sometimes it may be necessary to go to the individual product level in the breakdown. When starting to build a company model for the first time, it is better to err on the side of more detail, such as individual product volume, customer breakdown, and geographic breakdown to ensure an in-depth understanding of the company. Over time, the model can gradually simplify the less important parts of each segment and keep details only on the critical parts. In some cases, forecasting segmental revenue by end market and market share, as opposed to product segment, can give a better picture of the direction of the business. Including a segmental revenue breakdown in the model is an important foundation, ensuring an understanding of the business and also improving forecast accuracy.

Income Statement Forecast

Once the segmental revenue is created, analysts should move to the income statement. The key here is to first come up with the appropriate operating profit (EBIT; Earnings Before Interest and Taxes), a core figure in the income statement, and then add various other items to generate the net income forecast. It might be a helpful exercise to create a waterfall chart that shows all the key positive and negative factors driving the changes in operating profit each year for the past 10 years or so. The factors would typically be changes in volume, pricing, raw material cost, fuel cost, labour cost, rent, depreciation cost, R&D cost, sales and marketing cost, currency rate, product mix, and accounting method. Reviewing the historical figures will give a very clear idea of what moved the earnings of the company and also offer a good indication of how an analyst should forecast its future earnings.

Operating Leverage

For many companies, one of the most important points in the income statement forecast is the concept of operating leverage, hence it is worth digging deeper on this. Operating costs consist of variable costs and fixed costs, with variable costs moving along with sales volumes while fixed costs do not. Hence, if a company has low variable costs versus revenues and high fixed costs versus revenues, the profit growth is higher than revenue growth, assuming no increase in fixed costs. This can be quantified using contribution margin (marginal profitability; 1 – variable cost/revenue). For example, assuming a company has revenue of $100mn and operating profit of $20mn with 40% contribution margin, then if revenues go up by $10mn next year (driven by sales volume increase), the operating profit will be $24mn, assuming fixed costs will stay the same. This means when revenue grows 10% year on year, operating profit grows 20%. This operating leverage obviously works the same way in reverse when revenues go down.

Although companies do not normally disclose precise contribution margins, through detailed income statement analysis and company interviews, an analyst should be able to gauge an approximation of its contribution margin. The figure varies depending on the cost structure of a business, it is desirable to know the contribution margin of all key businesses if a company has multiple business lines. Companies with low fixed costs generally show a lower contribution margin. Companies with high fixed costs tend to show a higher contribution margin. Companies with minimal variable manufacturing costs, such as pharmaceutical and software companies, tend to have very high contribution margins. The baseline contribution margin should stay at a similar level over time, so it is a good starting point for earnings forecasts, but other factors discussed in this chapter, such as pricing, currency, and changes in costs, can influence the contribution margin. More structural changes, such as product mix changes and business restructuring, could also influence the contribution margin.

Product Pricing

Product pricing is a factor that can significantly impact a company's profitability. For example, assuming: 1) a company has a revenue of $100mn and an operating profit of $20mn, 2) that it will raise product price by 10% next year, and 3) that volumes stay the same, then revenue would be $110mn next year and operating profit $30mn, assuming all other things are equal. So, pricing impact is quite significant to profitability. In this example, the impact on profit is higher than in the previous example, which was based on a volume-driven revenue increase. Assuming 40% contribution margin, the volume-driven 10% revenue increase would lead to a 20% operating profit increase while the price-driven 10% revenue increase would lead to a 50% operating profit increase. As product price hikes can often be catalysed by cost inflation, the impact does not always fully flow through to the profit. But it is helpful to remember product pricing has a significant impact on the profitability.

Exchange Rate

Exchange rate is another significant item that can impact profitability. If a company has a substantial gap in revenue currencies and cost currencies, as is often the case for auto companies and airlines, then earnings can be significantly impacted when the exchange rates of those currencies fluctuate. The most sensitive companies can have c.2–3% operating profit impact per 1% move in the relative currency rate. Companies often make comments that the impact is small due to their hedging, but it would be unusual to see a company fully hedge their exposure for multiple years. So, the impact could be realized in the following year if not in that year, and the hedging is not free. The earnings impact driven by the gap between revenue currency and cost currency should be distinguished from a simple translation impact (i.e. a company's ADR-based (American Depository Receipt) earnings per share (EPS) can be revised when the US dollar exchange rate versus the local currency moves).

Changes in Cost Items

Earnings of companies that have large cost items, such as feed stock, labour, rent, fuel, can be substantially influenced by the fluctuation of those costs. Sectors such as energy, chemical, metals, retail, and transport, can be particularly sensitive to those changes. It is important to pay extra attention to these cost items during an inflationary environment. It is also important to monitor a company's efforts to mitigate such cost inflation through various efforts such as long-term contracts of rents or material sourcing. Well-managed companies can sometimes provide upside surprise on the ability to control costs. Some companies address this issue through upstream integration, i.e. steel producers buy iron ore mines, which might work during a period of raw material shortage but is not always a desirable strategy from a long-term asset return perspective. In the past, some airline companies had long-term contracts to anchor fuel costs, but ended up with sizable losses in later years due to a subsequent drop in oil prices.

Take Rate

In the online space, take rate means how much the online company can retain of its revenue out of the gross transaction value. It typically ranges from c.2–4% but could be between 0% and 10% depending on the nature and phase of the business. In online businesses, transaction volumes generally grow rapidly, 20–30% per annum, and companies need to navigate the balance between customer acquisition and profitability. In most other businesses, a higher margin is a good thing but in the online business too much monetization (meaning a higher take rate) could damage the pace of customer acquisition. So, analysts need to model the take rate with balanced considerations. One additional thing to note is that analysts need to distinguish between the 1P (first-party relationship) and 3P (third-party relationship) e-commerce models and treat them separately when modelling businesses. This is because 1P recognizes merchandising sales value as revenue and 3P recognizes just the commission fee as revenue, hence the margin profiles are very different.

Customer Acquisition Cost

Customer acquisition cost means the total marketing costs and discounts applied to acquire certain customers divided by the number of customers acquired by the effort. The concept is regularly discussed by companies in online businesses or software businesses and is often the source of earnings fluctuations for high-growth companies. The customer acquisition cost may be difficult to calculate just from a company's publicly disclosed data but is a useful discussion item when speaking to the company's management.

Depreciation Cost

It is useful for analysts to understand the full details of a company's depreciation policies and compare it with those adopted by industry peers. Differences in depreciation policies could have a significant impact on the earnings and thus they need to be equalized to enable proper peer comparisons. When a company is in a steady state, capex and depreciation should be roughly equal and steady. But when a company increases its capex rapidly or reduces it suddenly, the depreciation cost can change as well. If there is a significant change in capex, it is useful to build a separate capex model to forecast depreciation expense more precisely.

Research and Development Cost

High technology and biotechnology companies normally have high R&D costs, typically at least 10–20% of revenue. A good starting point for analysts is to assume the ratio stays at the same level going forward. But, as most of the R&D costs are ultimately personnel costs, if the model shows a 50% per annum increase in R&D costs in the next three years, there needs to be a reality check about whether they can actually hire that many R&D personnel so quickly. Some software companies capitalize part of R&D in the balance sheet as an intangible asset. When comparing the profitability of such companies with others, analysts will need to adjust the capitalized portion of R&D.

Inventory Fluctuation

Although inventory fluctuation is a rather temporary and technical issue of accounting as opposed to a fundamental issue, it is still useful for analysts to look at when reading financial statements. If demand for a certain product suddenly goes down but the manufacturer keeps up production at normal levels to maintain utilization, the unsold portion of products would go to its inventory and the calculated cost of goods sold (COGS) is allocated on a normal per unit fixed cost basis. So, in a way the COGS is artificially lower compared to its lower sales level. If the company lowered production level according to the demand reduction it would have an allocated higher per unit fixed cost, meaning higher COGS. Therefore, in the first scenario, the gross margin of the particular quarter would be higher than the underlying health of the business. If demand picks up quickly, the company can work through the inventory and have no prevailing issues. But if weak demand persists, the company will need to reduce the production level even lower than the demand later to work through the inventory and it would thus get hit by a higher per unit fixed cost. In this case analysts will see a higher-than-expected gross margin in the initial quarter or two and a tougher than expected gross margin in the subsequent quarters. In a worst-case scenario, the company might also have to take an inventory write down at the same time. The magnitude of this profitability impact would depend on the level of changes in the utilization rate and the type of inventory valuation method used.

Companies with Multiple Businesses

When analysing companies with multiple business lines, analysts need to work on all of the aforementioned processes for each business. The detail available on each division is unlikely to be as comprehensive as that available on the whole company. So, there will need to be a 'best-efforts' basis for analysts to come up with the divisional operating profit forecasts. Leveraging data from pure play companies in the same industries is critical. Meeting with the division heads is desirable to analyse such complex companies if possible.

Tax Rate

Each country has a different tax rate and a company basically pays the tax where they generate profit. If the majority of the profit is coming from one country, it is relatively simple to use the corporate tax rate of that country. Some countries offer special tax credits to some industries they want to promote but analysts need to examine how sustainable such special treatments are. Companies with a carried forward tax loss can use it as a credit for a specific period of time. Tax rates of multinational companies are inevitably hard to understand and forecast from the outside. However, what analysts can do is examine past tax rate fluctuations and try to understand the reasons behind those moves. Even though it is difficult to forecast the corporate tax rate of future years, it is worth spending time on this item because it has a substantial impact on EPS and free cash flow (FCF) forecasts.

Minority Interest

Minority interest is lower in the line items of an income statement but cannot be ignored as it can impact EPS, substantially in some cases. Analysts should closely monitor the profitability of any affiliates.

Dividend and Share Buybacks

In considering the total shareholder return, the cash dividend forecast is also important. When forecasting future cash dividends, analysts need to review the company's dividend policy to see whether it is aiming for a fixed dividend or progressive dividend. Some companies have a specific pay-out ratio target. In terms of share buybacks, if a company has a consistent buyback policy and that is significant, analysts could consider incorporating it into future share count forecasts.

Changes in Accounting Standard

Although it is a challenge to fully follow all the details of accounting standard changes, a high-level understanding of the major accounting standard changes of International Accounting Standards (IAS) and US Generally Accepted Accounting Principles (GAAP) in the past 20 years or so is helpful when analysing past financial statements. The areas of accounting standard often focused on by equity investors are items such as: 1) goodwill amortization and write-off, 2) employee share ownership plan (ESOP) expenses, 3) revenue recognition, 4) inventory recognition, 5) R&D expense, 6) lease expense, and 7) deferred tax revenue.

Earnings Guidance of the Company

Most public companies provide forward earnings guidance on some income statement items. Some only issue this for the next quarter and some for the full year. Analysts should not use them without examining the details. It is useful to understand why the company uses certain assumptions to come up with the guidance. Some companies are consistently conservative and some are consistently ambitious in the guidance provided. Analysts need to understand the guidance track record of the company in order to offer the best interpretation of the figures.

Balance Sheet Forecast

Once income statement forecasts have been generated, some parts of the balance sheet can be mechanically determined. There are also several major items that need to be considered when forecasting the balance sheet.

Working Capital

When thinking about the working capital management of a company, the following three numbers are important to assess: Accounts receivable (AR) days (account receivable/revenue x 365), accounts payable (AP) days (accounts payable/COGS x 365), and inventory days (inventory/COGS x 365). Normally, AR days are 100 to 150 days for regular manufacturing companies. However, if a company has customers with a long payment cycle, such as the government, the number can be closer to 300 days. In a cash business, like retailing companies, AR days are shorter. Inventory days typically run between 50 and 100 days for general manufacturing companies but if a company is in the long product cycle business, then this could go beyond 360 days. AP days are normally 50–100 days for general manufacturing companies and this reflects their bargaining power with suppliers. A larger AP days number is good for a company but it should not be at the detriment of suppliers and needs to be sustainable.

AR days plus inventory days minus AP days is referred to as the cash conversion cycle. When forecasting the balance sheet, a starting assumption is that those three numbers will be stable going forward. But if certain numbers have gone up or down in the past few years, and if there is a good rationale for that, analysts might use an ascending or descending trend. Those forecasts need to be tied to the business conditions. If a business is in trouble, the company might ask for a longer payment term with their suppliers, but if the company is in real trouble, then it might have to pay sooner. If a company has made significant efforts to streamline distribution channels, it might be able to reduce AR days and inventory days consistently. Or, if a company substantially improves the manufacturing process, inventory days can be shortened.

Fixed Assets

Property, plant, and equipment can be mechanically calculated by adding the capex amount to the prior year-end fixed assets and then subtracting the depreciation amount. If a company has relatively large fixed assets and a history of write-offs, analysts will need to understand the nature of these in detail.

Intangible Assets

If intangible assets make up a significant proportion of a company's balance sheet, analysts need to know the details, which in most cases would be goodwill from acquisitions. The health of the acquired businesses also needs monitoring to ensure no unexpected impairment losses are faced.

Debt Management

Once the asset side of the balance sheet has been forecast, how much debt a company needs is known. If a company already has outstanding debt, the maturity schedule of loans and bonds will need to be examined. If a company has floating rate debt or short duration debt, analysts need to run sensitivity scenarios around sharp rate hikes. Interest rates paid on this debt should reflect in the interest expense line of the income statement. If a company has a significant amount of foreign currency denominated debt, this could cause stress on the balance sheet if the foreign currency appreciates against the local currency. If a company is highly levered and the business is facing difficulties, in-depth credit analysis should be conducted, possibly with the help of credit analysts, to gauge the solvency of the company.

Cash Balance

When forecasting the balance sheet for cash rich companies, the cash position will be piling up every year. It is important to understand a company's general policies on cash position, shareholder return, and investment, to properly forecast the potential capital structure. If a company is acquisitive but it is difficult to factor future acquisitions into the forecasts, analysts can input a number into future capex as a proxy of acquisitions and add a similar level of return to that which the company has achieved with past acquisitions to the income statement.

Off-Balance Sheet Items

A common off-balance sheet item used to be operating leases. This becomes particularly important when looking at the industries with large leasing assets, such as airlines and retailing companies. But since 2019, all operating leases are required to be on-balance sheet, hence this is no longer a disclosure issue. The off-balance item that analysts need to pay attention to is off-balance sheet debt. For example, some property developers have debt under their subsidiaries as part of their projects.

Cash Flow Forecast

Once the income statement and balance sheet have been properly forecast, the cash flow statement should mostly be mechanically derived from them. Analysing historical cash flow statements can provide a lot of information about the nature of the business, which cannot be gained by just looking at the income statement. In particular, the cash conversion cycle is one of the critical aspects of financial analysis. No matter how good the profit margin and the asset efficiency are, a company's business might not be sustainable unless it can convert revenue into cash at a reasonable pace.

The cash flow statement is also a good place to do high-level cross checks regarding the quality of forecasts and whether they are balanced. For example, if the cash flow statement of Company A shows it keeps generating large sums of cash and that half of the balance sheet becomes cash in the fifth year of the forecast period, which is too good to be true, a few questions need to be asked as a reality check. First, check that the margin assumption that has been made is appropriate. Next, check that the capex level is sufficient to generate the levels of revenue, or whether the working capital assumptions are too optimistic. Then consider how the company could deploy the cash to ensure a more balanced capital structure.

Alternatively, if the cash flow statement of Company B indicates it will continue to burn large amounts of cash even though its income statement shows good earnings growth, a few questions need to be asked. For example, check whether the margin assumption is too low or the capex assumption is too high, or whether the company will improve its cash conversion cycle over time. If cash burn is highly likely, analysts should question how much room there is for the company to increase leverage or how much room there is for equity financing. Ultimately, the ability of the company to remain a going concern in the long term might come into question.

The key takeaway is that after all the forecasts have been generated, analysts need to look at the income statement, balance sheet, and cash flow statement to ensure they provide a cohesive story and meet the common-sense test.

How to Put Cyclicality into Long-term Earnings Forecasts

The issue of how to incorporate cyclicality was briefly discussed in the context of industry forecasts in Chapter 1. When forecasting five years of forward earnings for cyclical companies, it is likely that analysts will know from past patterns if there will be some kind of earnings cycle in the next five years. If that is the case, there are two possible methods when incorporating cyclicality into the financials. One way is to add explicit down years during the forecast period. This can be used for industries with relatively predictable cycles, such as capital goods and semiconductor equipment. Although it is not easy to forecast the precise timing, it is prudent to have explicit down years during the forecast period. The other method is to put the earnings forecasts in at the mid-point of the volatility range. This is potentially more suitable for the commodities or transport sectors where the cyclicality can be rather abrupt and random, and often driven by price swings. In a similar spirit, some oil sector analysts use long-term sustainable oil price assumptions when calculating the long-term earnings forecasts of energy-related companies, thereby avoiding potentially large swings in valuation if they were to incorporate the spot price instead.

Quarterly Forecasts can be Helpful

Even though long-term structural analysis is the main focus of this book, closely following quarterly industry data and a company's financial results are important in order to maintain high-quality earnings models. A new long-term structural trend can be picked up from the quarterly data. The key is how to distinguish between the short-term noise and the early signs of a long-term trend. In addition, analysis of year-over-year and quarter-over-quarter figures should give a good sense of the pace of potential earnings recovery in upturns or earnings decline in downturns. Analysts sometimes underestimate the pace of both directions, and quarterly numbers can be a helpful guide to temper that.

A Birdseye View is Helpful

If sector analysts just work in silos, they do not have a good enough relative sense of their sector. It is useful to look at aggregate sector level revenue and earnings forecast growth and then compare them against other sectors, especially ones with similar earnings profiles. Reviewing the historical cycles of these other sectors can also be informative.

Financial and Property Sectors are Unique

Financial statements of companies in the financial sector are completely different from most other industries and require separate training when learning how to read them correctly. The income statement is relatively straightforward but analysts need specific expertise to understand the dynamic nature of the balance sheet, such as asset and liability matching and capital requirements.

The property sectors, including REITs, also have very unique financial statements. They basically require the collection of details on all the major development projects and also details of the leasing assets. Given that most property companies finance their business with some leverage, the liability side of balance sheet analysis is important.

AUTHOR ANECDOTE

Story Needs to be Matched with the Numbers: Having reviewed tens of thousands of earnings models by myself, the most common issue observed in analysts' forecasts is a mismatch between equity stories and earnings numbers. An analyst may present a fascinating sustainable growth story on a sector-leading company with a strong competitive moat, but the model shows revenue growth forecasts from year one to five as 25%, 20%, 15%, 12%, and 10%. When questioned on why 25% growth is not used all the way to year five, the answer is usually that they are being conservative. Another analyst may talk about structural margin improvement in a sector due to consolidation, but the model of the leading company only shows the operating margin increasing from 20% to 21.5% in five years. When questioned about why the margin assumption is not 25% in five years, the answer is usually the same, they are being conservative. The point here is not to encourage analysts to be bold just for the sake of being bold, but to be honest about what has been learnt from their extensive analysis. It requires courage to forecast substantial margin expansion or strong revenue growth in the official forecasts, but if enough research has been done and the analyst believes in it, then not fully utilizing it in the earnings model is a waste of effort.

Where to
start

Err on the detailed side as
you start; simplify later ✔

Use earnings drivers to
construct the model ✔

Understand operating
leverage ✔

Understand the cash
conversion cycle ✔

The profit and loss statement, the balance sheet,
and the cash flow forecast ✔
should make a cohe-
sive story that meets the
common-sense test

What to
avoid

✘ Mismatch between the
model and the story – have
conviction in the figures

✘ Straight-line forecasting for
a cyclical industry

✘ Working in a silo – have a
relative sense of the sector

✘ Creating a model that takes
week to update

SOURCE: Goldman Sachs Global Investment Research

Chapter 5
Summarize All Thoughts

So far, in this book's process, analysts have gathered a vast amount of information and formulated thoughts on: the industry characteristics (Chapter 1), earnings drivers (Chapter 2), company personality (Chapter 3), and the financials (Chapter 4). It is now a good point to step back to summarize and digest what has been learnt and forecast. In most cases, companies are analysed in the context of peer comparison and now is a good time in the research process to form a comparative view. This can be achieved by creating a scorecard type table (see Figures 5.1 and 5.2). This process should help analysts to select and focus on the most important aspects of a company's performance.

A Suggested Method for Creating a Practical Scorecard

1. Select several items to represent industry characteristics, such as growth potential, competitive pressures, cyclicality, profitability, pace of changes, regulatory pressure. Similarly, identify

Figure 5.1   Sample company scorecard: industry characteristics.

Industry Characteristics	Industry X
Growth potential	**
Competitive pressure	**
Cyclicality	***
Profitability	***
Pace of changes	*
Regulatory pressure	*

SOURCE: Goldman Sachs Global Investment Research

Figure 5.2   Sample company scorecard: peer comparison.

Company Personality	Company A	Company B	Company C
Product quality	***	**	***
Distribution and marketing capability	***	**	**
Ability to innovate	*	*	**
Competitive moat	**	**	***
Awareness of environmental and social responsibility	**	**	***
Quality of governance	**	**	***
Financial metrics	**Company A**	**Company B**	**Company C**
Asset turn	**	***	***
Profit margin	**	**	***
Cash conversion	**	*	**
Earnings momentum	***	**	***
Earnings predictability	**	*	**
Balance sheet strength	***	*	**

Note: *** Above peer average; ** At the peer average; * Below peer average.

SOURCE: Goldman Sachs Global Investment Research

several items to describe the company personality, such as product quality, distribution and marketing capability, ability to innovate, competitive moat, risk management, awareness of environmental and social issues, governance quality. Several financial metrics, such as asset turn, profit margin, cash conversion, earnings momentum, earnings volatility, and leverage could also be picked. While each individual analyst can select appropriate sector items, it is important not to get too detailed and also to make sure the overall picture of the company is covered.

2. For the scoring method, use the simple designation of: three stars (***) above peer average; two stars (**) at the peer average; and one star (*) below peer average. If really needed, the scale could be increased to five, but three is enough in most cases in order to keep it simple. Analysts need to be objective in scoring and need to try to distribute the scores. If most companies are designated as **, the scoring is not useful. If it is really not possible to differentiate, the item can probably be omitted from the list. When deciding the scoring, analysts should, as much as possible, try to ensure a forward-looking perspective. There needs to be clear logic on how to score the company in each category.

3. Show a comparison with local peers and global peers separately if that is appropriate. Alternatively, it might be more appropriate to split the peer group by size or sub-category. Picking the right peer group is important to ensure the most relevant assessment of the company.

4. Once the scores are filled in, take a step back and glance at the whole thing to ensure it is coherent and plausible. Industry characteristics, company personality, and financials should all be interdependent. If the character of a company, as figured out through the research process, and the financial figures do not correlate, analysts need to ask why. Sometimes it may be necessary to go back and reassess and adjust some scores. In fact, the real value of having this scorecard is that it allows the analyst to glance at the findings and review them from a high level.

5. Total aggregated scores from the table can give some idea of which companies are positioned better or worse relative to the peer group. However, the main goal here is not to calculate the grade point average (GPA) of the company, and analysts should not be overly wedded to the overall scores. The more important point is that a company scorecard can help demonstrate research findings with clarity and also give the relative positioning against peers.

Where to **start**   ## What to **avoid**

Where to start		What to avoid
Form a high-level comparative view		Over-complicated metrics and relative scoring
Pick the right peer group to enable a sensible assessment		Non-differentiating metrics
Analyse from a forward-looking perspective		Mismatch between comparative results and fundamental thesis
Run the coherence test		Being overly wedded to comparing total scores

SOURCE: Goldman Sachs Global Investment Research

Chapter 6
Find the Appropriate Valuation Framework

Chapters 1 to 5 discussed how to understand a company better and in more depth. We now turn towards viewing a company through the capital market lens, i.e. how to look at a company's valuation. The valuation will represent all the aspects of a company, such as cash generation ability, asset efficiency, growth potential, management quality, franchise strengths, technological advantage, and brand value (see Figure 6.1). A company's valuation is generally expressed through relative value – typically price to earnings multiples compared to an appropriate peer group. Depending on the nature and the stage of the company, the market may look at its near-term earnings only or at the long-term trajectory of the earnings. An intrinsic valuation approach, such as discounted cash flow (DCF), could be used to supplement the relative value approach, if necessary, given certain conditions.

Valuing a public company using mainly company-specific fundamental financials is a challenge because the actual stock price can be driven by a number of other non-financial factors. In addition,

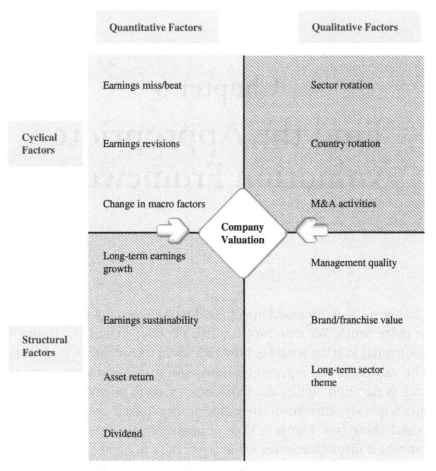

Figure 6.1   Key factors that can influence company valuation
SOURCE: Goldman Sachs Global Investment Research

equity market earnings multiples can largely be driven by interest rates, inflation rates, and economic conditions. However, this chapter aims to provide sector-specific valuation frameworks based on the company-specific financial data.

Broadly speaking, different valuation methodologies should give more or less the same result. Analysts should always be reminded that what is put in the valuation model (i.e. the earnings forecast) is the most important input that determines the quality of the output: garbage in, garbage out.

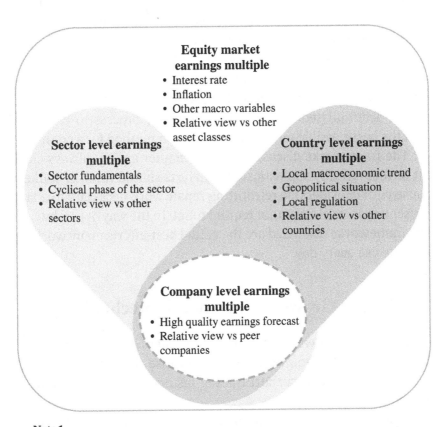

Equity market earnings multiple
- Interest rate
- Inflation
- Other macro variables
- Relative view vs other asset classes

Sector level earnings multiple
- Sector fundamentals
- Cyclical phase of the sector
- Relative view vs other sectors

Country level earnings multiple
- Local macroeconomic trend
- Geopolitical situation
- Local regulation
- Relative view vs other countries

Company level earnings multiple
- High quality earnings forecast
- Relative view vs peer companies

Note 1
Bullet points under each multiple describe the major factors that influence the respective multiple

Note 2
'Earnings multiple' is used to represent the valuation method, but the same idea can be applied to other methodologies as well

Figure 6.2 Company earnings multiples are influenced by multi-layered factors. *Equity analysts can add most value through high quality earnings forecasts, and relative views vs peer companies.*

In reality, valuing a company is a lot more art than science. Some companies have various business lines with different growth profiles. Some companies own large assets not related to their core business. Some new companies have a business domain in between two sectors. Some companies can be very acquisitive. Although, in principle, a company value can be derived by comparing it to relevant peers, it is rare for analysts to have the luxury of five or more clean identical comparable companies in the same stock market. Hence, analysts are required to leverage all the knowledge and insight accumulated through their research process to come up with the best-possible tailor-made valuation method for a company.

The frameworks discussed in this chapter are not always clear cut or theoretically sophisticated. Analysts should think of it like a house with considerable retrofitting repair work necessary to adapt to user needs, or clothes that require much in the way of patchwork. The frameworks discussed are the actual best-efforts many working analysts use every day.

Hyper Growth – Internet, Biotechnology

Valuing hyper growth companies (consistent top-line growth of 25–30% or above) requires creativity because they often have new business models with a short trading history and it can be hard to find comparable companies.

When dealing with companies without profit (sometimes without revenue), analysts will need to use a DCF model as the primary methodology. DCFs are typically run using a forecast period of 10 years, but if there is a particularly strong long-term growth scenario for the company then a two-stage or three-stage DCF with 20–30-year earnings forecasts can be applied. Discount rates normally range from 11–12% for high-risk businesses to 8–9% for medium-risk businesses. But this could go up to 15–18% for a company with an unclear business model. Terminal growth typically ranges from 1–3%, depending on the company's growth profile post the forecasting period. In high-growth countries 4–5% terminal growth may be used on rare occasions. There is no theoretical formula to calculate the discount rate and terminal growth numbers that should be applied, but those discussed are used in practice and tend to fit well with the market valuation. In order to somewhat mitigate the black box nature of DCF, the key is to use consistent assumptions across similar types of companies and then the discount rates and terminal growth assumptions should not be changed unless the long-term growth outlook or risk profile of the company or sector changes materially.

When using DCF to value hyper growth companies, it is a good idea to have a second look at the key assumptions in the associated earnings model, such as penetration rate, market share, MAU, ARPU, take rate, working capital, to make sure all findings from the qualitative analysis are reflected in those forecast numbers.

When valuing companies based on profitability, it can be based on the 5th to 10th year forward EPS with the industry average P/E used as an exit multiple. This value would then be discounted to the current fair value using an appropriate discount rate. The exit P/E multiple can be either the historical regional sector average P/E or the historical global sector average P/E, assuming the hyper growth companies will eventually be valued at an industry average P/E when growth rates moderate. DCF, enterprise value (EV)/Sales multiples, and price earnings to growth (PEG) ratios, are also used to value hyper growth companies with profitability, but each has its own shortcomings, hence they should be used with other methodologies to cross check.

Some high-growth internet companies have profitable core businesses and loss-making new businesses at the investment phase. If an analyst has strong confidence that those new businesses will turn profitable in the future, they could be valued separately to avoid unnecessary dilution of the value of the healthy core businesses. DCF or discounted P/E (using a 5–10-year forward EPS) based on the potential margin such new businesses could earn, can be used to value them.

Secular Growth – Software, Medical Technology

Sectors such as software and medical technology typically demonstrate consistent high top-line growth with a sustainable high margin. As a result of this combination of high growth and a reliable margin profile, the market tends to assign premium earnings multiples to those companies.

To capture the high-growth potential, these companies can be valued based on the 5th to 10th year forward EPS with the industry average P/E used as an exit multiple and then discounted back to impute the current fair value. This exit P/E multiple in the final year can be either the regional sector average P/E or the global sector average P/E, assuming the high-growth companies will eventually be valued at an industry average P/E when their growth rates normalize. If the industry average P/E has been stable over time, that could be used. If the industry average P/E is ascending, the recent figures may need to be used to ensure the current market environment is reflected. Such exit multiples can differ depending on a company's growth potential post the forecast period. If this growth potential exceeds the industry average, it could make sense for the exit multiple applied to be higher than the industry average. DCF is also a commonly used methodology to value such high-growth companies and it would be useful to cross check the DCF result with the 5th to 10th year forward P/E method as described.

For emerging software companies, although not giving a specific fair value, the comparison of CAC (customer acquisition cost: annual increase of recurring revenue divided by the annual sales and marketing expense) and LTV (life time value: total gross profit value during the product life time) can help gauge the health of the business.

Cyclical – Capital Goods, Transport, Energy, Commodities, Chemicals, Autos

Valuations of cyclical stocks move in parallel with the earnings cycle. Such valuations often fluctuate above or below the potential intrinsic value of the company. Valuing cyclical companies has a different nuance than valuing stable growth companies. For stable earnings companies the aim is to measure an absolute value to represent the intrinsic value at that time. But, for cyclical companies, the valuation approach discussed here is about finding the valuation range of the companies in the different earnings cycle phases.

When cyclical companies are in the downturn of the cycle, they are either making a loss or have lower profitability, hence earnings-based multiples become unusable. So, the historical trough P/B (price to book) level is often used to gauge the potential share price floor of the current cycle. If the business environment is particularly weak, and there is a risk of asset impairment, analysts also need to look at adjusted book value after the asset impairment cost.

When the cycle is in an upturn, cyclical companies can grow earnings very quickly and are very profitable. In order to gauge the potential share price upside, analysts can look at potential peak earnings of that cycle and apply a cycle average multiple (P/E or EV/EBITDA), because peak cycle value rarely reaches the level of the peak earnings on peak multiple. If available, it is better to use consensus earnings when calculating historical earnings multiples, to avoid perfect foresight bias. If using perfect foresight earnings (the actual historical earnings), P/E charts often spike up not because the stock went up but because the earnings disappeared suddenly. By the time that spike has happened, the stock price starts to reflect P/B multiples or forward earnings, and ignores the depressed earnings. Therefore, although it is not perfect, using consensus earnings at that time can at least give the P/E multiple the market was assuming at that point in time.

In the cyclical sectors, more so than for any other sectors, the key is that analysts need to revise forecasts swiftly and boldly as the stocks move fast and a delay means being behind the curve.

So far in this section, a company's historical multiple range has been used to provide a context for the valuation of a cyclical company. In addition to a company's own historical P/E, EV/EBITDA, and P/B multiples, sector average multiples should be used to cross check the valuation level.

Some auto companies have sizable financing business on their balance sheet. Analysts will need to analyse the financing unit separately in that case.

Cyclical Growth – Semiconductor, Technology Hardware, Clean Energy

The valuation framework of cyclical growth companies is similar to the one used for cyclical companies. When the companies are in a cyclical downturn and the earnings are depressed, P/B is often used to gauge the valuation floor. When they are in a cyclical upturn, potential peak earnings forecasts and mid-cycle multiples are used to gauge the potential cycle peak valuation. There is no scientific reason why analysts must use the mid-cycle multiple but, for companies operating in a cyclical industry, it is a useful number to help to anchor the outlook as the multiple often gets to the mid-cycle multiple but rarely reaches the peak multiple on peak earnings.

Unlike pure cyclical companies, however, cyclical growth companies are unlikely to hit historical trough P/B multiples during the downturn, given that the market likely anticipates the next strong upcycle. During the upturn, the real key is to accurately forecast the next peak earnings level, which could be higher than the prior peak. Analysts can apply cycle average multiples to the next peak earnings forecast to gauge the peak valuation of the cycle. As discussed in the cyclical section earlier in this chapter, it is better to use consensus earnings at the time when historical earnings multiples are being calculated, to avoid perfect foresight bias.

Stable – Consumer Staples, Retail, Consumer Discretionary, Pharmaceutical, Media, Business Services

Assessing the valuation method of stable earnings companies is not as complex as those mentioned earlier in this chapter. Sector average multiples are relatively constant historically and companies tend to carry similar multiples within the same sector. Therefore, valuing stable earnings companies using the sector average multiple (either P/E or EV/EBITDA) of a forward year is a good place to start. If certain companies have been consistently carrying higher or lower multiples versus the sector average, analysts can add such a premium or discount to the valuation, although before doing so the historical premium or discount needs analysis to understand why it has occurred. Companies with better margins and asset returns tend to exhibit valuation premiums as long as those high returns are sustainable. Companies with relatively stronger competitive moats, such as brands and patents, can also carry premium valuations.

If the sector has companies with different levels of capital structure, EV/EBIDTA might be a more appropriate method to use. However, care should be taken as the fair value can be very volatile when using EV/EBITDA multiples for highly levered companies. When using enterprise value for companies, any off-balance sheet assets will need to be added to net debt.

Given the models of most pharmaceutical companies are built based on long-term sales forecasts of major drugs, DCF can be used for the valuation together with near-term earnings multiples. DCF will be particularly helpful when companies have major new drug launches or patent expirations in the outer years.

Some emerging market companies that belong to this industry category can have consistent high earnings growth. When analysing such companies, in order to capture their growth potential, the valuation can be based on the 5th to 10th year forward EPS with the industry average P/E used as an exit multiple and then discounted back to impute the current fair value. This exit P/E multiple in the final year can be either the regional sector average P/E or the global sector average P/E of developed countries, assuming high-growth companies will eventually be valued at an industry historical average P/E when their growth rates normalize.

Interest Rate Sensitive – Banks, Emerging Market Banks, Insurance, Property, REITs

Interest rate sensitive sectors, such as property, banks, and insurance each have unique and widely used valuation methodologies.

Banks

Banks are valued in a continuum, typically in conjunction with economic cycles. In normal to upward trending economic cycles, banks are typically valued on an earnings multiple, P/E, price to pre-provision operating profit (P/PPOP), or dividend discount model (DDM). Asset light recurrent fee income businesses (for example wealth management) are normally valued at a premium to asset heavy balance sheet lending. The earnings multiple applied is related to earnings growth and sustainability of returns, typically return on equity (ROE, where P/B divided by ROE = P/E), with premiums and discounts factoring in relative growth, profitability, and business construct.

Recall Chapter 2: asset heavy bank earnings growth is a function of capital build and so a high sustainable ROE leads to the ability to support lending growth, which in turn generates higher returns. As the cycle turns down and pro-cyclical earnings decline, or even head to losses, valuations shift to balance sheet measures of P/B. When capital is compromised with a deep cycle crisis, valuations may move to an intrinsic measure of franchise value, such as price/deposits, or price/adjusted book (adjusted for any anticipated capital raise to restore capital to minimum levels).

Emerging Market Banks

Emerging market banks may be valued using similar methodologies as developed market banks but differences in implied multiples may be explained by lower industry penetration and higher industry growth, and where relevant higher interest rates that accompany higher economic growth. Given the number of factors that drive the valuation continuum, and the relative valuation methodologies, it may be helpful for analysts to combine the various drivers and weight the score as a fundamental beta to help derive the cost of capital. The CAMEL ratings system for example is sometimes used by regulators to assess the relative positioning of a bank through the core categories: Capital, Asset quality, Management, Earnings, and Liquidity.

Insurance

Life insurance is one of the few products sold where the cost is only understood after the life cycle of the product is complete and fully utilized, and where the profitability of the product has a very long duration and grows over time. To capture these unusual characteristics, a long duration estimate of the profitability of the cumulative portfolio is forecast, namely in the Embedded Value calculation, which is the insurance equivalent of a DCF. However, in recent years the entire valuation construct has fallen into question given the numerous and changing assumptions with consequent large changes in the Embedded Value. Therefore, the market has shifted towards earnings and dividend-based multiples for the more mature markets.

For the short tail property and casualty (P&C) insurance businesses, more typical valuation methodologies are used, such as P/E, P/B versus ROE, and dividend yield.

Property

Most non-REIT property companies have a property development business and a property leasing business. To value such property companies, net asset value (NAV), which is the summation of all the present value of development projects and leasing assets, is widely used. In theory, a property company's value should be equal to its NAV, similar to the concept of DCF, but a premium or discount can be added depending on the prospects for the property market in that region or the execution track record of the company. In some emerging countries where the property business is still a growth business, like China, landbank is relatively small and the development cycle is short, and there may be insufficient projects to calculate NAV. In that case, flow earnings methods such as P/E can be used to supplement the valuation.

REITs

Given its fixed income-like nature, a REIT is almost solely valued using its dividend yield. As it is a domestic business, the dividend yield should be compared against other REITs in the same equity market. The sector average dividend yield should be correlated with local interest rates and the difference in dividend yield among individual REITs is likely driven by several factors such as strength of its sponsor, financial position, quality of the asset, category of the asset, and track record of asset acquisitions.

Regulated – Utilities, Telecoms

Given the protected nature of their cash flow due to the oligopoly structure of the industry, regulated sectors such as telecom and utilities can be valued based on a combination of dividend yield, EV/EBITDA multiple, and FCF yield. Companies can be valued based on their historical range and peer comparisons. Since the business is mostly domestic in nature, peer comparisons should be done within those companies listed on the same stock market.

In Europe, many utility companies are rushing to invest in renewable energy business, such as wind and solar, to mitigate their carbon footprint. As such, analysts should use DCF and sum-of-the-parts to add the value of those new businesses into the valuation.

For telecom companies, which face major spectrum auction charges, given new entrants in the market and other potential future earnings disruptions, DCF should be deployed to supplement the dividend yield and EV/EBITDA multiple methodologies.

Conglomerates

When a company owns various different businesses, analysts will need to use a combination of different valuation methodologies suitable for each business. Although each business line might not have sufficient disclosures compared with pure play companies, a best-efforts basis can be made by leveraging peer comparisons. Conglomerate companies normally carry a holding company discount, which means the market value is lower than the total value of the individual assets. This discount typically ranges between 15% and 45% and the reasons behind such a discount are widely believed to be a lack of transparency, cohesive strategy, and business synergy. Although it is arbitrary, when considering the holding company discount, analysts should compare it against other conglomerate companies with a similar structure and business mix. The track record of the companies on asset recycling and capital optimization should also be a factor considered when calculating the holding company discount to be applied.

Figure 6.3 Sample valuation framework by sector

Hyper Growth – Internet, Biotechnology	• DCF (non-profitable companies) • P/E (profitable companies): 5th to 10th year forward EPS with the industry average P/E used as an exit multiple • DCF, EV/Sales, PEG can be used with caution and with other methodologies to cross check
Secular Growth – Software, Medical Technology	• P/E: 5th to 10th year forward EPS with the industry average P/E used as an exit multiple • DCF
Cyclical – Capital Goods, Transport, Energy, Commodities, Chemical, Autos	• Historical trough P/B: To gauge the potential share price floor of the current cycle • P/E or EV/EBITDA: To gauge potential share price upside using potential peak cycle earnings and applying a cycle average multiple
Cyclical Growth – Semiconductor, Technology Hardware, Clean Energy	• Historical trough P/B: To gauge the potential price floor of the current cycle • P/E or EV/EBITDA: To gauge potential share price upside using potential peak cycle earnings and applying a cycle average multiple • Key is to forecast how much higher the next peak earnings could reach versus the previous peak

Figure 6.3 (*Continued*)

Stable – Consumer Staples, Retail, Consumer Discretionary, Pharmaceutical, Media, Business Services

- P/E or EV/EBITDA: Sector average multiple of a forward year
- Add premium or discount if evident by historical trend and/or if there is a justifiable reason
- Exercise caution if applying EV/EBITDA for highly levered companies

Interest Rate Sensitive – Banks, Insurance, Property

- Earnings multiple (P/E, P/PPOP, DDM) for banks in positive economic cycles, and Price/Book during negative economic cycles
- Embedded value calculated for life insurance companies
- Price/Book versus ROE, and dividend yield for P&C insurance businesses
- NAV for property companies
- Dividend yield for REITs

Regulated – Utilities, Telecoms

- Combination of dividend yield, EV/EBITDA multiple, and FCF yield
- Valuations, based on historical range and peer comparisons
- DCF and SOTP should be deployed to supplement dividend yield for utility companies

(Continued)

Figure 6.3   (*Continued*)

Conglomerates	• Combination of different valuation methodologies suitable for each business
	• Best-efforts basis to leverage peer comparisons with pure play companies

SOURCE: Goldman Sachs Global Investment Research

Additional Considerations on Valuation

High and Low Multiples

Different industries trade on quite different earnings multiples. Even within the same sector, some companies trade with a premium and some trade with a discount. The difference in the multiples can be explained by medium-term growth rates, earnings reliability, home market valuations, balance sheet quality, liquidity of the stock, strength of the corporate group, brand, etc. Although difficult to quantify, it is desirable for an analyst to have their own views on why certain sectors or companies carry high or low multiples versus others, rather than simply taking the market value as it is.

Analysts sometimes make a comment on the de-rating or re-rating of a company's valuation but when doing that they also need to have a good idea about what is driving the valuation multiple changes. In some cases, some countries have a consistent valuation discount or premium versus other markets. For example, within Asia, the Korean market tends to carry lower earnings multiples, which can be attributed to the corporate governance issues faced by large company groups. The Indian market tends to carry higher earnings multiples, which could be attributed to its higher economic growth. However, even within those markets there is a wide variance of valuation multiples among different sectors. Companies in cyclical sectors typically carry lower valuation multiples than the market average due to earnings cyclicality. In some rare cases, a perceived cyclical company can turn itself into a secular growth company due to the transformation of its business model and thus the valuation may re-rate to higher levels. Whether high-growth fintech companies should be valued in between banks and e-commerce, given the ongoing and evolving regulatory restrictions, is an interesting debate.

How to Choose Comparable Companies

When using a peer multiple approach the selection of comparable companies makes a material difference in the valuation results. The simplest way is to use peer companies in the same industry in the same market. But if Company A has global business exposure and the rest in the industry are domestically focused, then it is more suitable for Company A to be valued against global players in different markets. Or, as discussed in Chapter 1, some industries are converging and thus analysts need to add different aspects into the valuation. For example, if a capital goods company is increasing the proportion of earnings from its recurring service revenue, some premium can be added to its valuation for its earnings sustainability versus peers. The size of the company is another consideration. A company with $10 billion revenue is very different in nature to one with $500 million, even if they belong to the same industry, and they might need to be valued separately or require some adjustments to valuation based on the difference in market cap size or trading volume derived from the valuation history.

CROCI

CROCI is calculated as debt adjusted cash flow (DACF) divided by gross cash invested (GCI). It aims to measure a company's cash flow generation ability per accumulated dollar invested in operating assets. CROCI can provide a clear picture of the earnings power of a company, especially for companies with physical assets, and it can compensate for the shortcomings of ROE or return on invested capital (ROIC). As touched on in Chapter 1, if CROCI is broken down into three elements: 1) asset turn (revenue/GCI), 2) profit margin (EBITDA/revenue), and 3) cash conversion (DACF/EBITDA), it will be easier to understand the strengths and weaknesses of the company. As for the forecasts, CROCI dilutive earnings growth can result in valuation deterioration because it means the company's incremental investment has a lower return. Those that can sustain or expand to high CROCI would likely maintain high valuation premiums. Industries where the major companies cannot generate CROCI above their WACC (weighted average cost of capital) will likely go through consolidation. High CROCI industries can attract new entrants. CROCI is also helpful to assess whether certain acquisitions by the company are dilutive or accretive from an asset return perspective.

PEG Ratio

When analysts value high-growth companies, the PEG ratio (P/E divided by EPS growth) is sometimes used because it is simple and intuitive. It is an easy cross check tool to use but cannot be used without thought. For example, when an analyst cuts earnings forecasts, if the fiscal year 0 number is cut more than fiscal years1–2, the growth rate goes up and a higher P/E will be applied. This does not make sense. Instead, the 'G' of PEG should conceptually be thought of as the sustainable growth of the company. If the use of PEG as a main valuation methodology is wanted, analysts need to make sure the industry actually demonstrates a positive correlation between earnings growth and P/E, and that earnings growth is relatively consistent for multiple years.

Reality Check

The is no one valuation methodology that is perfect. As such, it is helpful to compare different methodologies to cross check the results. In particular, when using more complicated methodologies, such as sum of the parts (SOTP) valuation and DCF, to generate fair value, analysts can make rough top-down comparisons of the company with similar types of companies in the same market or global peers in the same industry by using metrics such as P/E, EV/EBITDA or Price/Sales ratio.

Residual Value

When valuing businesses that are profitable in the near term but could face significant structural headwinds in the long run, using a long-term DCF with no residual value can be useful. Businesses such as internal combustion engine cars, coal fired power plants, and digital cameras are likely to be profitable for the next few years but a discount applied to the valuation may be appropriate given the long-term sustainability risks.

Scenario/Sensitivity Analysis

Earnings estimates of cyclical companies tend to be very sensitive to volume and pricing assumptions and can swing, with quite a wide range. Hence, on top of a point estimate, analysing the lowest and highest possible outcomes in certain scenarios is very useful in gauging risk and reward versus the current stock price. The key is to have an appropriate range of assumptions, ensuring they are wide enough but also realistic at the same time. Scenario analysis is also useful for non-cyclical companies where the earnings can be influenced substantially by unpredictable binary events such as changes in regulation and geopolitical issues. Alternatively, it is also useful to plug the current stock price in the model and extract the level of growth rate and profitability the public market is implying for the company.

Back Test

To gauge the suitability of a certain multiple-based valuation methodology for a particular sector, the data should be put into a scatter plot chart to see if there is line of best fit. Alternatively, an actual stock performance back test using historical share price to compare several different methodologies can be useful in the selection of more suitable valuation methods. But, given share prices are driven by many other factors besides financial performance, spending too much time on small differences of back test performance is probably not overly productive for the purposes of company analysis discussed in this book.

M&A Value

When the market looks at certain companies as acquisition targets, sometimes those companies can trade above their fundamental value due to the acquisition premium driven by a variety of factors. If needing to put such a premium into the fair value calculation, analysts can calculate the potential M&A value of a company based on historical acquisition multiples of past transactions in similar sectors and then add that to the fundamental fair value using an appropriate probability weighting such as 15%, 30%, or 50% (analysts will need to use their own judgement, based on an array of factors, to determine the likelihood of a company being acquired). So, if the probability of a company becoming an acquisition target is assumed to be 30%, the adjusted fair value is the total of 70% fundamental value and 30% M&A value.

Sector-level Relative View

From time to time, it is helpful to see the sector valuation from a top-down point of view. Comparing the current average valuation (P/E, EV/EBITDA) of Sector A versus various other sectors, or comparing where the current valuation percentile of Sector A is within the historical range versus other sectors, should give a fresh perspective. If several other sectors are indicating valuations at the 70–80th percentile versus the history, and Sector A is showing at the 30th percentile, analysts should question why.

Where to start

Identify a suitable methodology ✔

Use common sense ✔

Learn to use CROCI ✔

Run a scenario analysis to gauge risk reward ✔

Triangulate the valuation using an alternate method ✔

What to avoid

✘ Taking the market multiple 'as is' – analysts should have their own view on multiple value

✘ Underestimating the importance of an appropriate peer group

✘ Using valuation methods like PEG and EV/Sales without thought

✘ Perfect foresight bias

✘ Talking about valuation 'de-rating' or 're-rating' without considering structural changes in earnings trajectory

SOURCE: Goldman Sachs Global Investment Research

Chapter 7
Differentiation versus Street

High-quality company research work is valuable in itself. But an out-of-consensus view based on high-quality research work is far more valuable in the investment process. An analyst discovering the difference between the proprietary view generated by their own work and the market consensus is a rewarding part of company research as it completes the whole process of research work. To crystalize the value of those differentiated views, analysts should articulate clearly in their research where and why they are different from the market view, and should continue to monitor progress of the differentiated thesis. As differentiation from the street can be a vague concept, this chapter provides tools to help analysts put some structure to this.

Is the View Actually Different?

How does an analyst know whether their view is different from the street or not? There are three possible ways:

1: The Fair Value Conclusion is Different to the Current Share Price

This is the most straightforward one. But a company's share price can sometimes be influenced by factors beyond fundamentals, such as the sudden liquidation of a stake by major shareholders, and occasionally the calculated fair value can differ versus the current market price even though an analyst's fundamental view is similar to the market view. The key here would be to try to gauge the factors the current share price is discounting.

2: The Earnings Forecasts are Different

Readily available consensus data is generally sell-side analysts' earnings numbers aggregated by third-party information providers. But consensus can sometimes be lagging, especially when fundamentals are changing fast. So, although it is difficult, efforts need to be made to gauge the 'real' street consensus earnings through regular communication with key investors.

3: The Equity Story is Different from the One the Market Believes

Although this one may seem pretty vague compared to the other two, it is still important. If the conclusions about the 'personality' of a company following the whole research process are different from those recognized by the market, then the view is differentiated. It is very useful to have a good dialogue with major active shareholders of the company about their view.

Where is the Difference?

If an analyst believes their view is different from the street, specifics should be provided when explaining where that difference is located.

- **Core areas**: Relatively near-term normal modelling variables, such as sales volume, pricing, input cost, sales and marketing costs, capex level, production yield could be driving the difference.
- **New businesses**: The difference could come from the longer-term assessment of new business areas the company is trying to grow. As a result of the comprehensive research undertaken, an analyst may have a more optimistic or pessimistic outlook on some new technology or service than the street.
- **Risk assessment**: Difference versus the street could be driven by a broader risk assessment on the company's execution, regulatory environment, competitive pressure, product obsolescence, etc.

What is Driving the Difference?

Having identified specific areas where their view may differ from the street, analysts should then articulate the driver of those differences.

- An analyst may have reflected certain macro-condition changes or industry-environment changes into earnings more quickly than the market. Not all information is discounted by the market immediately.
- An analyst may have a higher conviction on a known trend, hence incorporating bolder estimates than the street. Detailed work undertaken throughout the research process can sometimes give analysts high conviction. Everyone likely agrees that online penetration of many businesses will increase over time. But if the market expects the penetration rate of a certain product to be 15% in five years and original research from the analyst concluded that it will be 20% in five years, the view is very different.
- Discovering something the market has not yet acknowledged. Bottom-up analysis can sometimes lead an analyst to pick up something counterintuitive. For example, when construction activities are in a downtrend due to a slowing economy, many would think the demand for construction machinery would go

down. But it may actually stay strong because of labour shortage and tighter emission regulations.
- An analyst may discover an attractive company that is less well known by the market. These high-growth companies can typically be found in the small- and mid-cap space and are generally not widely covered by sell-side analysts.

Value of an Undifferentiated Conclusion

Even if the research conclusions of an analyst are not differentiated versus consensus, and in the majority of cases they won't be, high-quality research work, such as good industry forecasts, clear understanding of the earnings drivers, clean earnings models, a thoughtful valuation framework, and extensive people network, will not be wasted. These can become extremely valuable when the stock price of a company moves or industry conditions change. Truly differentiated company analysis only happens when an analyst has a high-quality original view on a company, an in-depth understanding of the market consensus, and when those two differ. It does not happen very often and that is why it is so valuable.

Where to **start**	What to **avoid**
Communicate with market participants as much as possible ✔	✘ Believing aggregate consensus estimates without question
Think deeply about where the analysis is different – not just the numbers ✔	✘ Underestimating the value of quality research due to an undifferentiated conclusion
Articulate where the difference is originating ✔	✘ Underplaying your conviction view just to be 'conservative'
Monitor progress of the differentiated thesis ✔	

SOURCE: Goldman Sachs Global Investment Research

Part IV

What to Research and How to Power the Analysis

Chapter 8
How to Generate Exciting Ideas

So far, this book has mostly focused on the 'how to' part of equity research but it is equally important to think about 'what to' research in order to discover new themes and attractive companies. Research topics for new analysts are often provided by their managers. Even so, after going through the basic research steps, there is a myriad of ways to add a fresh angle to the research. Below are nine suggestions to help analysts come up with new ideas and interesting companies.

1: Burning Questions

Trying to look for answers to 'burning questions' is useful because if it is still a question then that means many people do not have a clear answer. The advantage, over other professions, of being an equity analyst is the ability to quantify such questions. Journalists can discuss these burning questions but might not always be able to provide quantitative answers to them. Academics and international organizations can sometimes provide forecasts in response to these questions but updates to their data may not be sufficiently frequent, thus they may be of limited use for company analysis. For example, with the pressure of decarbonization mounting everywhere, one of the burning questions in the energy industry relates to the long-term future of oil demand and the timing of its peak. A team of equity analysts can come up with legitimate long-term oil demand forecasts by leveraging the help of various sector teams, such as autos, transport, solar, power generation, industrial, and macro. Putting a small mosaic together to quantify and answer burning questions is something all equity analysts should try.

2: Products to Solve Problems

It is often surprising how quickly products or services, which can solve problems of individuals or companies gain traction. For example, although it ended up with the bankruptcy of some of the companies involved, at its conception the bicycle sharing business addressed the frustration of commuting in highly populated cities. In office life, regulatory technology solutions or digital document signature services can address daily frustrations at work. So, looking at problems and frustrations that surround us and then finding products and services to address them can be a useful exercise.

3: Forgotten New Technologies

Equity analysts can sometimes be very excited about certain new technologies and conduct extensive research on those topics for a while. But in a situation (which happens in many cases) where the new technology does not grow quickly enough to become an earnings driver of the company in the near term, analysts often stop focusing on it because they have many other things to deal with every day. While they are 'forgotten', some technologies could steadily make progress on performance improvement, cost reduction, new usage creation, etc., and emerge as a formidable new business. Technologies such as silicon carbide (SiC) wafers (used to produce high-performance semiconductor chips), virtual/augmented reality, and 3D printing might fall into those categories. Although analysts may not have the time to follow all of the potential technologies all the time, it is sometimes helpful to revisit the 'old inventories' of past research themes and see whether they have made any major progress.

4: 'Little Stories'

Many interesting ideas could come from little stories told by your friends, industry contacts, colleagues, etc. Sometimes hints are hidden in specialized industry periodicals or news articles. How to pick up those and connect them to research ideas is up to the creativity of an analyst.

AUTHOR ANECDOTE

Recently a small news article caught my eye on the use of wood to create wind turbines for power generation. I never thought such equipment could be produced from wood and the article immediately got me thinking about a number of areas. What were the implications for wind turbine companies, for other heavy machines (i.e. their potential to use wood), for steel demand, for the forestry industry, etc.? I am clearly exaggerating the potential impact of this example but the key point is that even small hints can generate interesting research ideas.

5: New Language

Many interesting ideas can be picked up by just being a consumer or an office worker. But to go further, an analyst will need to learn the basics for certain technical industries. It is difficult to hold a decent conversation on software companies without knowing the variety of new concepts of the industry. It is very difficult to talk about semiconductor manufacturing process without knowing how a transistor works. It is difficult to conceptualize the new business opportunities of NFT (non-fungible token) or DeFi (de-centralized finance) without understanding the basic mechanism of block-chain. But the flip side is that once a basic knowledge and understanding of the technical side has been gained, whole new areas of opportunity will open up. It is similar to the experience of learning new languages.

6: B2B and Orphan Stocks

An area in which there is less competition to find new ideas is B2B. Everyone can experience a new hotpot restaurant and it is not hard to understand the concept of service quality. But it requires relatively more work to understand the market for reflective paint material used in traffic signs or the market for reduction gears used in industrial robots. Those highly specialized companies with a dominant share in small market segments can be very attractive. Additionally, companies generally not analysed within the traditional sector coverage (orphan stocks) have a higher chance of being overlooked.

7: The Second or Third Derivatives of Structural Changes

Many people will look at the structural changes for new ideas, but to go beyond that, analysts need to explore the second and third derivatives of them. For example, single-use plastic has been under attack from many fronts. But thinking more broadly about the entire carbon footprint versus using alternative materials, the discussion point might shift from 'should we use it?' to 'how recyclable are they?'.

8: Local Trends

Some products or services that have become very popular in one country are worth watching. There should be a good reason why people in the country like it so much. It might not happen immediately, but with some catalysts it could spread to other countries quickly. Bubble tea and short-form video apps are recent examples of this.

9: Inputs from the Real World

Sometimes people who engage in capital market activities have a particular way of viewing the world. The tendency can be to see countries and companies through the lens of GDP size, capital market size, and trading volumes, and there may be nothing wrong with that approach because that is where the business opportunities are. But there are a number of populations and economic activities in the world that have been ignored by mainstream global capital market activities.

AUTHOR ANECDOTE

When I attend conferences like the World Economic Forum, it is eye opening for me to realize the gap between the 'real-world' view of the world and the view from the financial industry. Topics receiving a lot of traction in capital markets recently, such as clean energy, plant-based food, education technology, income inequality, disaster recovery, genomics, data privacy, cyber security, have been widely discussed in such forums for many years. It is useful for those of us in the financial industry to get some input from the 'real world'. I was quite surprised to observe how quickly hydrogen energy related businesses had gained traction among equity market participants in the past one to two years. Although the technology had been around for many years, the sudden increase in low carbon policies by countries outside Europe catalysed various large public companies to start talking about the technology and the equity market then followed. Plant-based food is potentially another example. If society starts to scrutinize the carbon footprint of fishery and livestock farming businesses, companies who are involved in fish and meat products might be forced to transition into plant-based foods, similar to the way oil companies are required to invest in renewable energy. The Japanese fishery company I wrote my first research report on might have to produce plant-based crab meat to survive in the future. It might not taste perfect now but if enough companies spend ample resources, the quality should improve quickly, as seen with many other similar developments.

Where to **start**

What to **avoid**

Where to start		What to avoid
Look for the 'burning questions'		Sticking with traditional sector categories
Find products and services that solve a problem	✔ ✖	Ignoring the 'little stories' while waiting for a 'big idea'
Gather ideas from everyday conversations and anecdotal stories	✔ ✖	Misunderstanding the domino effect of structural changes
Align thoughts to the real-world issues	✔ ✖	Being afraid of technical terms

Chapter 9

How to Deal with Disruptors, Emerging Markets, ESG, and Downturns

In addition to the key research process discussed in the earlier chapters of this book, this chapter seeks to address some often-asked questions regarding company analysis.

How to Forecast and Value 'Disruptors'

Digital transformation, genome revolution, decarbonization and various other innovations are producing a number of 'disruptors' – companies that drastically change the landscape of incumbent businesses – and they are increasing their presence in the market. Such disruptors typically demonstrate very high top-line growth and low or negative free cash flow for many years because of the heavy burden of capex, customer acquisition cost, and R&D cost. The following content may be somewhat repetitive of the hyper growth discussion in Chapter 6 but this section of this chapter has been created to address this market segment, which is growing in importance. It is important to note upfront that forecasting and valuing such disruptors is not an easy task, with even the most experienced analysts struggling to do so. Hence, the points discussed describe the industry's best-effort practices.

Forecasting the Earnings of Disruptors

In principle, the process of analysing disruptors should not be very different from the way other companies are analysed. However, many of the basic research processes discussed earlier in this book become even more critical because disruptors are growing fast and changes are more significant than in other more mature industries. It is much like driving a racing car where the sensitivity of the steering wheel and pedals is very high, and where even a little movement by the driver can result in a large move by the car compared to regular cars. There are four key points analysts should focus on.

1: Top-Down TAM Forecasts

To capture future business opportunities, analysts need at least 10-year forecasts. An important point when calculating the TAM is that it should be done from a top-down perspective. The business of the disruptor often replaces incumbent products or services. If online grocery penetration will go from 5% to 50%, the portion of TAM will become 10 times greater. Sometimes analysts begin the TAM forecasts with 20–30% CAGR (compound annual growth rate) by extending the past growth, but potential rapid acceleration of growth could be missed when using that approach. Analysts need to have the courage to forecast certain markets becoming 10 times greater in 10 years, with their conviction backed up by solid research.

2: Market Share Forecasts

Since the focus is on forecasting for the long term, competitive dynamics might change over time for high-growth businesses. Better understanding of key competitors' strategies and deliberate market share forecasts based on the analysis, as opposed to defaulting to the current market share, is very useful.

3: Balance Sheet and Cash Flow

Analysts need to make sure capex, R&D cost, customer acquisition cost, and working capital assumptions are sufficient to achieve rapid top-line growth. Detailed discussions with companies and peer comparison of data are necessary to understand how much investment is needed to achieve certain revenue growth assumptions. Some high-growth companies use negative working capital effectively to fund their growth, while some may struggle due to a heavy working capital burden.

4: Margin

High-growth disruptors can be unprofitable during the investment phase but they cannot lose cash forever. Toward the end of the forecast period, analysts need to forecast the post investment phase margin to gauge the ultimate earnings power of a company. For example, online businesses often provide services or products at a loss to gain customer traffic and associated data, based on the assumption that such customer base and data will yield a substantial profit in the future. As such, analysts should seek to quantify the potential profit margin when the company fully monetizes such data from the customer base and put it in the earnings model.

How to Look at the Valuation of Disruptors

DCF

DCF valuations have a number of shortcomings. However, when it comes to valuing disruptors, DCF is inevitably the most suitable method, since many of these companies have very high revenue growth and almost no near-term profitability. In order to mitigate the criticism of DCF being a black box, analysts can try to have relatively consistent modelling assumptions versus peers with similar business dynamics within a broader sector. As discussed in Chapter 6, discount rates of 10–12% and terminal growth rates of 1–3% are commonly used DCF assumptions depending on the risk and growth profiles of the companies in question. As a cross check, analysts should also try to look at the valuation implied by using 10th year forward EPS multiplied by the broader sector average P/E. While it may be obvious that no one can accurately forecast company earnings (or in fact anything) for the next 10 years, the ambition here is to quantify all knowledge gained on the company at this stage and come up with a best-efforts-based proxy of the company's intrinsic value.

Scenarios

Given the uncertainty surrounding various assumptions in the model for future years, it can be useful for analysts to discuss valuation ranges. For example, analysts could have three or four different valuations based on different scenarios where key variables are flexed. They can then somewhat gauge what the current stock price may be discounting by comparing it to the valuation range. If the main scenario valuation is substantially different from the current market value, analysts should think about why this is the case. When the market for a stock looks 'hot', analysts sometimes need to resist the temptation to simply justify current stretched market valuations by applying a higher multiple, instead having the courage to stick with their own assessment of fair value.

Maintenance

The operating environment of disruptors could change quickly. As soon as an analyst picks up a new development in the industry or with the company, it should be reflected in the long-term forecasts.

How Should Emerging Markets be Looked at?

To find attractive growth companies, emerging markets are the natural place to go. However, it is sometimes misleading to look at emerging market companies through the lens of developed markets. Emerging markets consist of many diverse countries and it is hard to generalize them but there are a number of common characteristics that analysts need to be aware of, five of which are discussed here.

1: Terminology

When referring to a certain product or service in English in an emerging country, it might refer locally to a fairly different product or service. For example, a few years ago in China, what people called 'yogurt' often actually meant a sweet drink with a yogurt taste that can be preserved at room temperature and that has a higher sugar content than many types of cola. So, if an analyst claims the yogurt market can grow fast in China due to the increasing health consciousness, this will need to be questioned. In India a few years ago, products that were called 'insurance' actually often meant very short duration wealth management products. So, it is always important to clearly define terminologies to avoid confusion.

2: Things Can Move Much Faster

When analysing the long-term outlook of an industry in emerging markets, examples from developed countries that have been through similar paths are often used. But sometimes, although not always, the progress of emerging countries can be much faster due to the second mover advantage, technology advancements, etc. The e-commerce adoption curve, adoption of health-conscious foods, and adoption of cashless payments are a few examples among many.

3: Lack of an Apparent Cohesive Strategy

When examining the business models of companies in EMs, sometimes they are found lacking in clear strategies. Some start four or five different new businesses at the same time, some change the core business every three years, some make acquisitions far from their core areas. It can be confusing at the beginning when coming across these situations, even for listed companies. But once analysts become more accustomed to those companies, it will likely become apparent that a number of companies are quite successful over time despite the lack of consistent strategies. In many EM countries the market moves very fast, competition is fierce, and funding is abundant. Hence, companies just need to move very fast to grab the large growth opportunities in front of them.

4: Comparison among Emerging Countries

Global comparison is critical for good-quality company analysis and it is even more important when looking at EM companies. Many markets in EM countries are relatively small with limited listed companies and often there are only one or two in the same industry. In order to analyse those companies from multiple dimensions, comparing them with similar companies in the markets of other emerging countries is very useful. For example, comparing the business models and competitive landscape of the food delivery business globally is very informative as each country has a slightly different industry structure.

5: Government Subsidy

In some countries governments grant subsidies for their preferred industries in the forms of cash grants, tax credits, investment credits, R&D credits, etc. In some cases, this can contribute a substantial part of their profit for many years. There is no clear answer to the question as to whether a discount should be applied to the portion of profit generated from subsidies. But at a minimum, analysts should be aware of why such subsidies are given to companies and how sustainable they are.

How to Think about ESG Issues

The focus on environmental, social, and governance (ESG) issues in the investment community has intensified in the past few years, and it is becoming increasingly difficult to talk about company analysis without considering ESG issues. There are numerous debates and differing views on how to approach ESG issues as part of the company analysis. In the following section, five items that should help an analyst formulate their thoughts on this important topic are discussed.

1: Definition

One of the more confusing aspects of ESG is its definition. Ask 10 finance professionals about their definition of ESG, and most likely there would be 10 different answers. Focus can be on CO_2

emissions, corporate governance, circular economy, and employee wellbeing. Some may think of it as a process to exclude negatives, such as tobacco and coal, while others view it as a philosophy to improve the quality of corporate management. All of the above are true, but to avoid confusion there needs to be clarification on which specific point of ESG will be discussed before getting into this topic in a meeting, presentation, or research report.

2: ESG Data

ESG data is an important tool in providing an objective basis for company level ESG discussions. However, it should be understood that most ESG data is still in the early stages of development due to incomplete disclosure and a lack of standardized definitions in individual data. Much of the governance-related data is actually policy statements rather than quantitative data. Therefore, at the current juncture, it is risky to rely too much on such data to judge the overall quality of a company's ESG efforts. But if a gap can be identified between the perceived quality of the company versus its relative ESG score, it can be interesting to explore the reasons. In the past few years, significant effort has been made in this ESG data area by corporates, investors, and regulators, and it will likely only accelerate from here. New generation analysts in particular, given they have a longer residual life as analysts, should take this trend very seriously and invest time and effort to fully understand and monitor it.

3: Corporate Social Responsibility

Given that the main objective of private companies is to pursue their own profit, how much social responsibility the society should expect of these companies is a debated topic. It is fair to say the social norm seems to be moving toward expecting more responsibility for corporates to perform good for the society across the countries in which they operate. In the consumer staples and apparel industries, some ESG aspects, such as reduction of single-use plastic and recycling of materials, are directly impacting their branding, especially with younger consumers.

4: Business Opportunities

ESG could be a short-term cost burden for some companies, but can also create attractive long-term business opportunities. The commercial viability of emerging business opportunities, such as hydrogen technology, carbon capture technology, recycling business, equal employment opportunity compliant software, alternative meat, agricultural technology, biodegradable materials, and electric arc furnaces are likely to increase. Those technologies have existed for some time but tighter regulations and changes in consumer behaviour could lift the scale and profitability of those businesses over the coming years.

5: ESG Valuation

Whether analysts should add a premium or discount to a company's valuation multiple based on their approach to ESG or not is another debatable question. Regarding relatively obvious businesses under ESG scrutiny, such as coal mines and tobacco producers, analysts can explicitly factor in long-term earnings pressure due to higher taxation and declining demand. Whether a valuation premium should be added to a company that is achieving very high recycling rates of its products, or a company that has a best-practice governance structure, is still unclear. The easy answer is that those qualitative aspects could be reflected in the company's future earnings stream positively if the analysis is properly done, hence an implicit premium on near-term multiples may be given to those companies.

But in the future, as the quality of ESG data improves, analysts might be able to add some valuation adjustment based on a company's ESG qualifications.

AUTHOR ANECDOTE

I recently attended a top management speaker session of major global consumer product companies. Key points of discussion were: 1) the importance of sustainability issues in their current businesses; 2) although most consumers think sustainability is important, they do not want to pay for it, thus companies need to mitigate the cost hike associated with sustainability efforts through collaborative innovation; and 3) given the wide scope of sustainability issues, companies need to set priorities to achieve maximum impact. I was deeply impressed by the level of detailed knowledge and commitment regarding sustainability issues by the top management of large corporations. The discussions also made me think about how analysts should measure such efforts by the companies given they are generally less visible. When I used to cover three office copy machine companies 15 years ago, one company was substantially ahead on recycling efforts versus the other two. However, back then, very few investors or analysts, myself included, paid much attention to these recycling efforts. It was not clear if customers of the copy machines could even distinguish the difference.

However, the level of awareness has changed markedly since then. It is worth analysts monitoring how such efforts could influence the market share gain of that company going forward. It is not a new concept that the stock market can look through near-term earnings dips due to aggressive customer acquisition costs, higher R&D, or higher capex for growth. So,

AUTHOR ANECDOTE (*Continued*)

when the stock market acknowledges that more evidence of sustainability efforts can have a positive longer term financial impact on a company, a valuation premium might be realized. Investors can even accelerate the company's sustainability effort through proactive engagement. It is also very interesting to find that even the large, established global consumer product companies cannot solve sustainability issues by themselves. Hence, enabling technology or services to support recycling activities should generate significant business opportunities.

How to Cope with Economic Downturns

Every few years, analysts come across severe economic downturns. When that happens, the first thing equity analysts need to think about is to cut earnings forecasts quickly and sharply to align the earnings forecasts with the reality. Analysts always prefer to have hard confirmation data before they revise down numbers, but in such sudden economic shock periods, numbers need to be cut based on a bold top-down judgement. What needs to be considered is not only the primary impact but also the secondary impact. The chain reaction of changes needs to be thought through – sales volume, product pricing, inventory level, working capital, financing cost, capex, input costs, consumption, etc.

While an economy is still falling, the conundrum of analysts is even though they want to cut earnings numbers they cannot do it without explicit assumptions of macro numbers and surrounding industry forecasts. A useful tool in this situation is 'hard landing scenario' analysis. Research heads can set pessimistic, but realistic, macro assumption scenarios, which sector analysts then use to come up with the most pessimistic earnings forecasts for their companies, but all based on the same macro scenarios for consistency. As these forecasts are scenarios and not official earnings forecasts, analysts are less reluctant to put in bold numbers. Once the macro scenarios and potentially the worst earnings of the cycle have been incorporated, it should be relatively easy for analysts to gauge what the current market level is discounting.

Another challenge is forecasting the recovery. If the downturn was deep, recovery tends to be steep as well. Analysts, especially cyclical analysts, should quickly change their mindsets from recession to recovery as soon as the cycle has passed the inflection point, and then work on earnings recovery. The operating leverage analysis is critically important to forecast earnings swing during this type of environment, both on upside and downside swing.

Where to start

Start with bold top-down approach to forecast 'disruptors' revenue ✓

Define the scope clearly in advance when discussing ESG matters ✓

Make substantial earnings cuts swiftly when economic downturn emerges ✓

What to avoid

✗ Simply justifying current market valuations of disruptors without consideration

✗ Always expecting cohesive strategies from EM companies

✗ Assuming a certain English term has the same meaning across different countries

SOURCE: Goldman Sachs Global Investment Research

Chapter 10
Using Soft Skills to Power the Analysis

How to Build a Relationship with Companies

One of the most important elements of an equity analyst's job is to build a high-quality relationship with companies and other industry contacts. There are a number of things that can help build a strong industry network, three of which are discussed here, although these are also common sense and applicable to any human relationship.

1: Trust

As part of the research process, analysts sometimes need to publish negative commentary on a company. Sometimes analysts may make mistakes in the analysis. To earn trust from companies, it is critically important to be fully transparent about what analysis has been done, and to be intellectually honest about it, all the while maintaining close communication with management during the difficult period. This is especially true when a company is in a vulnerable position. Rather than just writing about how difficult the situation is for that company, analysts should instead discuss potential paths for it to take to turn around the situation, which is beneficial analysis both for the company and investors.

2: Mutual Benefit

If analysts meet their company or industry contacts and just keep on asking questions, the relationship is unlikely to last long. Successful analysts often give more to their contacts than they take, with the result being these contacts are eager to meet such analysts. In fact, analysts can offer many very useful things to companies, such as investor feedback, high-level industry views, insights from other industries, and also macro views relevant to the industry. If an analyst wants to build a network of industry experts outside their coverage companies, this 'give-and-take' relationship becomes even more critical.

3: Passion and Preparation

Those analysts considered outstanding in their field tend to be extremely passionate about their coverage industries. If a genuine interest is shown in their business, products, services, or technology, companies will normally open up and welcome analysts. To demonstrate the enthusiasm and respect necessary, ample homework is needed. This is especially true when meeting engineers or scientists, where the extra mile on preparation can yield much better information. When meeting senior management, analysts can start by asking questions related to their areas of expertise. For example, if a CEO is originally from a marketing background, start a conversation about the company's new marketing campaign rather than the detailed technology of new products. Asking about success stories in the company's past often gives an analyst the opportunity for longer and more substantive conversations, full of hints regarding the corporate culture.

How to Leverage the Team

The benefits of team collaboration have been mentioned in many parts of this book. This section provides some ideas on how analysts can best leverage the knowledge and expertise of their colleagues.

1: Share Questions

The starting point is to share information as much as possible. Similar to the corporate relationship, it should be a 'give-and-take' relationship. Share with them and this will be reciprocated over time. Sharing something interesting with relevant analysts after coming back from corporate meetings is good practice. But what can be more effective is to solicit questions from team members before meeting with the company contacts. For example, when securing a meeting with the head of 5G technology at a leading telecom equipment company in Europe, which is probably hard to get, analysts should solicit questions they want to ask in this meeting from global analysts who cover the telecom and telecom equipment companies. Afterwards, the meeting notes should be shared. By doing this, not only do analysts improve the quality of the prepared questions, it also increases team knowledge about 5G and promotes team spirit. It may appear to be a small thing, but can have a positive impact, especially if everyone makes it a habit.

2: Form a Temporary Cross-Sector Group

Many industry themes are complex and one analyst or even one sector team cannot handle it by themselves. What needs to be done when researching such themes is the formation of a small cross-sector temporary group to tackle the subject within a short period of time. Handling this as a project is an effective approach. For example, when doing deep dive research into tourism consumption, the primary analyst should form a temporary group to discuss the theme with European luxury goods analysts, Hong Kong REITs analysts (i.e. those covering the high-end malls), Korean cosmetic analysts, and Chinese airlines analysts. Although it is deemed joint work, the primary analyst should be prepared to do the majority of the work to get the project done. Generous credit sharing of the project is key for the success of any future collaborations.

3: Casual Chats

As most analysts tend to specialize in one area quite deeply, having regular forums with analysts from different areas to casually share what they are seeing and hearing can be very useful. When inflation pressure is creeping into the economy, it is useful to know if multiple analysts in different sectors are seeing early signs of price hikes, for example. The pattern recognition discussed in Chapter 1 can be constructed during such conversations.

4: Debate

Sharing information is a win-win situation and is straightforward. But sometimes analysts need to debate and make a tough decision. When needing a conclusion on which companies are gaining and losing market share in the next five years, and two analysts have conflicting views, resolving this is not an easy task. Although it is painful, such debate should not be shied away from because it will generate lots of useful insights. The more teams share information and the tighter the relationships are, the better the quality of such discussion will become.

5: Joint Presentation

Sometimes the best occasion to learn from other analysts is when making joint presentations either internally or externally. People tend to give 120% when they are in front of clients and that environment could generate very creative ideas.

How to Communicate Ideas Effectively

Although this is not an item on company analysis itself, great analysis can only be complete with effective presentation. The six tips identified can be particularly useful for analysts when making an impactful presentation in just a few minutes under time pressure.

1: Conclusion First

In the financial industry where time is extremely precious, always use the format of conclusion first and then points one, two, three, etc., when speaking. During the question and answer session, always start with the short answer, such as yes, no, or figures. In many cases, a lengthy explanation of why the answer is 'yes' might not be necessary.

2: Provide Context

It is very helpful to tell people why the topic is important and why it is being talked about now. Analysts often miss this because they are so deeply involved in the topic and so interested in it that they assume other people automatically understand and are interested in it too. But other people need an explanation as to why the topic is so important before getting into all the details.

3: Know the Audience

This is related to the context point. Before speaking, analysts need to understand the knowledge level of the audience on the topic and also areas of interest in relation to it, adjusting the commentary according to those needs.

4: Use a Few Key Numbers

Numbers are a powerful tool for conveying messages. Use two to three punchy numbers during a short presentation so that people can remember them. If they do not remember them then those numbers are not so effective.

5: Difference from the Street

As discussed in detail in Chapter 6, it is critical for analysts to articulate where and why their view is different from the consensus. If the view is in-line with the consensus, analysts should question whether it is worth making the pitch.

6: Listen Carefully

Analysts should listen carefully to any questions they are asked, to try and fully understand exactly what is being asked. Not directly answering a question can be very frustrating for listeners. A good question and answer session is often more memorable than the quality of the presentation itself.

7: Chain of Thought

During an interactive meeting, it is important that presenters respect listeners' 'chain of thought'. Every audience has their own sequence of comprehending new ideas. Once the listeners start asking questions, analysts should follow their sequence of logic as opposed to the analyst's sequence of logic.

What Types of Training Should New Analysts Ask for?

On top of self-help and experience, new analysts definitely need further training to reach senior analyst levels. Rather than just waiting, analysts should proactively ask their managers for suitable training programmes. So, what type of training could be most helpful?

1: A Deep Dive Research Project

It is strongly recommended that analysts undertake a super deep dive research project into one company. Without a specific deadline, analysts can go as deep as they would like to test intellectual limits. Following the advice given in Chapters 1 to 6 should ensure a comprehensive understanding of the company. It will also require extensive regular check-ups and guidance from the analyst's manager to make it work, thus their cooperation is critical. The quality and depth of this first major research project will somewhat define the character of the analyst.

2: Peer Presentation

Groups of new analysts can get together regularly to present whatever materials they are working on at that time and question each other. This can provide tremendous benefits for those on the giving and the receiving end. Analysts need to have a deep understanding of the subject matter in order to explain it well to non-experts. When listening to other new analysts presenting, it may be clear to the listener where the pitfalls of the logic and analysis are. As peers, analysts should be pretty direct and honest with each other about feedback, without the concerns of being judged by seniors.

3: Critical Thinking Projects

New analysts should proactively put up their hands to take part in group discussions. These groups are usually formed with the intention of honing skills to think deeply and critically, and can take the form of three to four new analysts discussing simple big picture topics such as 'What is going to happen to the office building market in a post Covid-19 world?' After several hours of discussion and some fact findings, these groups then present their ideas on the topic to a broader group, with senior analysts sometimes taking the role of moderators and challengers. For new analysts, the challenge is how to find original angles from this pretty plain topic and how to create thoughtful conclusions. The most important takeaway from this critical thinking project is that analysts learn how to keep asking 'why' several times to certain statements until they feel they cannot

AUTHOR ANECDOTE

Python Training: I would not pretend I know anything about computer coding. But given the increasing amount of data we need to handle during the research process, for the new generation analysts, I would recommend getting yourself familiarized with skills for using software such as Python (a programming language) to be able to handle data efficiently. I still remember my first boss refused to use any spreadsheet software and was modelling on a sheet of paper instead.

go any deeper. This exercise does not need to be done often, as those skills are also learnt on the job, but it is sometimes good to participate in concentrated training to refresh the brain.

Time Management

Time management is one of the toughest issues almost all analysts face. It is particularly difficult for new analysts who are learning how to do the job and have relatively less control over the workflow compared to senior analysts. Although there is no easy solution, the four points discussed can help with how to approach this issue.

1: Timetable

After being assigned a project, it is a good idea to create a weekly level timetable. Working as an analyst usually requires frequent travelling and external appointments, thus detailed schedule planning and monitoring are important. As there will be multiple tasks being worked on at the same time, it is important to consider in advance how to manage schedule conflicts. Every morning, before starting to read emails and news, take five minutes to look at the calendar and think about what should be achieved in the day as a priority.

2: Management of Managers

It is important that new analysts properly manage their managers. They need to agree on deadline expectations, quality of the end product, potential workload, and prioritization of a project versus other projects. If the workload is too much, analysts need to discuss what can be cut from their daily work to make time. Managers can sometimes give tasks without fully considering the capacity of the analyst and it is a collective responsibility to flag any issues and come up with solutions. Constant and proactive updates for the managers and other stakeholders is key.

3: Research takes Time

New analysts need to understand that research takes time, as anyone who has done in-depth research work will know. If it can be done efficiently and quickly, it is an information processing task rather than real research work. Similar to scientific research, real in-depth company research requires a lot of hypothesis testing and hence takes time. It is important to ring fence some of the working day to think creatively about the project. Analysts need to learn how to handle the information processing side of work efficiently and accurately.

4: Quality and Depth First

If there is a trade-off between speed and volume versus depth and quality, new analysts should always go for the latter. An analyst's approach to, and style of, research is likely to be defined during their first few years and may not change much as more experience is gained. There is almost no value in mediocre quality research work, given how competitive the market is.

Where to **start**   # What to **avoid**

Where to start		What to avoid
Need mutual benefit to establish industry network		Not managing the manager
State conclusion first when presenting		Producing 'difficult to consume' research
Promote healthy debate – diversity of opinion enhances research		Compromising quality for speed
Form temporary project team to tackle new interesting themes		Waiting - proactively seek training opportunities

SOURCE: Goldman Sachs Global Investment Research

Part V

Recap and Closing Thoughts

HOW TO 'PREDICT' THE FUTURE OF A COMPANY: The Top 10 Dos and Don'ts extracted from key takeaways at the end of each chapter

Dos			Don'ts
Get on the road and visit	✔	✘	Turn to the model too early—lay the groundwork first
Hit the history books	✔	✘	Think only linearly—your job is to understand change
Define TAM properly	✔	✘	Misinterpret the incumbent's cynicism toward changes
Learn how to use pattern recognition	✔	✘	Overlook cultural and regional nuances
Know the earnings drivers	✔	✘	Have a mismatch between the model and the story
Identify the competitive moat	✔	✘	Take the market multiple as is—need to have your own view
Understand operating leverage and cash conversion cycle	✔	✘	Misunderstand the domino effect of structural changes
Run a scenario analysis to gauge risk reward	✔	✘	Use valuation methods like PEG and EV/Sales without thought
Articulate where you are different	✔	✘	Simply use aggregate consensus earnings numbers
Align yourself to the real-world issues	✔	✘	Underplay your conviction just to be 'conservative'

SOURCE: Goldman Sachs Global Investment Research

Closing Thoughts

Be **C**reative
Challenge the status quo, stretch your imagination, embrace non linear changes

Connect the **D**ots
Find patterns, identify trends

Be **B**old
If we do not put it in the numbers, good research will be wasted

Enjoy
Company analysis is a fascinating process, enjoy the excitement from new products, innovation, and stories of successful people

Ask why
Great research starts with good questions

SOURCE: Goldman Sachs Global Investment Research

About the Author

Shin Horie has 33 years of experience working in equity research. He is global cohead of Equity Research for Goldman Sachs. Prior to taking this management position, Shin was a technology analyst specializing in semiconductors and he also headed up the Asia technology business unit. Prior to joining Goldman Sachs, he covered China H-shares in Hong Kong and the capital goods sector in Japan at Nomura. Shin earned a BA in Law from Waseda University and an MBA from The University of Chicago. He enjoys travelling and speaks Mandarin and Spanish.

Acknowledgements

This book discusses the approach, methodology, framework, tips, and potential pitfalls regarding company analysis.

All the content included is derived from the tens of thousands of live conversations I have held with company managements, industry experts, investors, and analysts since starting out as an equity analyst in the 1980s. I would like to thank all of them for giving me a great deal of intellectual stimulation and enthusiasm, which has cumulated in the broad range of topics discussed in this book.

Thanks also go to colleagues in the financial industry who have read drafts of the chapters related to their areas of expertise and generously provided advice: Pippa Vizzone, Joy Nguyen, Kash Rangan, Amit Hazan, Julie Chou, and Rukhshad Shroff. I would also like to thank Brian Rooney, Juliet Mackinlay, and Juhi Malik for helping get this book into shape. Finally, I would also like to thank Madhav Rajan for his review of the draft and the invaluable feedback provided.

Index